LET NOT MAN PUT ASUNDER:

A STUDY OF MARRIAGE, DIVORCE, AND REMARRIAGE

By Tony Springer

© Copyright, 2018 Tony Springer
All Rights Reserved.

No portion of this book may be reproduced, stored in a retrieval system, or transmitted, in any form or by any means, electronic, mechanical, photocopying, recording, or otherwise without prior written permission from the author or publisher.

Print ISBN: 978-1-949215-00-7
EBook ISBN: 978-1-949215-01-4

Cover picture: Estefania solveyra-unsplash.com
Cover Design: Rory C. Keel

Printed in the United States of America

Published by
Carpe Diem Publishers
17401 Betty Blvd.
Canyon, TX 79015
806-433-6321
www.carpediempublishers.com

To my God for His love and kindness in
giving the gift of marriage to mankind.
To my wife, Wilma, a testimony
to His goodness (Proverbs 16:22)

PREFACE

I want to thank my wife for allowing me the time spent holed up in my office while writing this book. I am thankful that she did so without complaint and gave me her full support of this work. I am especially grateful to my nephew, Nathan Springer, for all the time and work he put into this book. I am grateful for his countless hours making sure all the quotes were properly credited and accurate, and making sure the spelling and punctuation is correct. I want to thank David Minson and Michael McCorkle for reviewing my book, and for their challenging questions and recommendations. I want to thank my son Rusty for his support and encouragement.

There have been few doctrines that have impacted the institution of family more than the doctrines taught on the subject of marriage, divorce and remarriage. My purpose for writing this book has little, if anything, to do with my personal family situation since I have been happily married for what can be numbered in decades, not just years, and I have only been married once. Also my children are all happily married and only once each. In addition, both my wife's parents and my parents were happily married until death parted them, neither couples having been divorced. My purpose for writing this book is simple; as an Elder especially, and as a Christian, I must be prepared to give an answer to everyone that asks a reason for the hope that is in me (1 Peter 3:15). The traditional doctrine on MDR, which I held for many years, seemed to have as many questions as answers. For this reason I had doubts about the doctrine, but because I knew nothing else, and since it was all that had been taught to me on the subject, there was no alternative but to accept it even though the traditional teaching did not pass what I sometimes refer to as the "smell test." For many years I ignored the subject, thinking some things may be too complicated to have a satisfactory answer for every situation and perhaps it is better to leave it up to God to sort them out. My advice at times was to give someone a few passages to read and tell them to decide for themselves what to do. That was certainly not satisfactory and not the way most other questions were handled. So I began to research the subject and found the traditional view was not the only perspective among those in the church of Christ. I also discovered that at one time in the history of the restoration movement it may not have been the view held by the majority in the church or at least (if it was) it was a small majority. Around the 1960's and 70's the traditional teaching on MDR became the prominent view and all other views were labeled "liberal" by recognized "leaders" in the church, who for the most part were in charge of most church publications. This labeling did two things, first: any opposing view was branded false without having to prove them false; second: it discouraged personal investigation into the truthfulness of the traditional view (after all, who wants to be labeled a liberal?). Having grown up in this period, the traditional teaching was all that was being taught in many places; all other perspectives were being suppressed. There were a few during this time challenging the traditional teaching, which cost them good standing among many in the church. Around the 1980's and following, some very bold and courageous men began to challenge the established teaching (in books, articles and lectureships etc.) and encouraged those in the church to lay aside preconceptions and take a fresh look at scripture in regards to the MDR question. As I began (in the mid to late 90's) to look into the subject from a different perspective than the traditional view, over the next several years there were some "aha" moments which occurred, and lights began to come on (metaphorically speaking). Overcoming preconceptions was a gradual and sometimes awkward process, and my understanding was certainly not well defined at various points in my journey as I began to transition away from the traditional perspective. Having come to a point where a high degree of confidence was obtained in understanding the teaching of scripture on MDR, a strong desire to share these discoveries and insights on this important subject developed. What you have in your hands is the result. I do not claim to have come to the right answer for every passage examined in this book as my understanding is an evolutionary process and subject to human error. The only claim (by this author) of infallibility in this treatise is being made in regards to the quotations of the inspired word of God. What you have before you now is my understanding of those infallible truths and I present them for your examination.

T. S.

Contents

INTRODUCTION..8

CHAPTER I: 14
GOD'S VIEW OF MARRIAGE

CHAPTER II:..20
THE "ONE FLESH" RELATIONSHIP AND WHEN A MARRIAGE IS A MARRIAGE

CHAPTER III:...32
ADULTERY, FORNICATION, AND "PUTTING AWAY"

CHAPTER IV:...54
THE SERMON ON THE MOUNT

CHAPTER V:..63
POLYGAMY AND JESUS' AUDIENCE

CHAPTER VI:...80
MATTHEW 19 AND "PUTTING AWAY" VERSUS "DIVORCE"

CHAPTER VII:..95
MATTHEW 19:3-9

CHAPTER VIII:..114
THE EXCEPTION CLAUSE, "PUTTING AWAY" VERSUS "ADULTERY," AND MARRIAGE ELIGIBILITY

CHAPTER IX:..131
1 CORINTHIANS 7 AND PAUL

CONCLUSION..164

APPENDIX A...166

APPENDIX B...169

BIBLIOGRAPHY...174

BIBLE VERSIONS...181

INTRODUCTION

Genesis 2:18-24 And the LORD God said, It is not good that the man should be alone; I will make him an help meet for him. And out of the ground the LORD God formed every beast of the field, and every fowl of the air; and brought them unto Adam to see what he would call them: and whatsoever Adam called every living creature, that was the name thereof. And Adam gave names to all cattle, and to the fowl of the air, and to every beast of the field; but for Adam there was not found an help meet for him. And the LORD God caused a deep sleep to fall upon Adam, and he slept: and he took one of his ribs, and closed up the flesh instead thereof; And the rib, which the LORD God had taken from man, made he a woman, and brought her unto the man. And Adam said, This is now bone of my bones, and flesh of my flesh: she shall be called Woman, because she was taken out of Man. Therefore shall a man leave his father and his mother, and shall cleave unto his wife: and they shall be one flesh.[1]

You will find that my view of marriage, divorce, and remarriage (MDR) is foreign to what is traditionally taught. I have come to the conclusion that the traditional approach is not the correct approach to MDR. When I use the terms "traditional approach" or "traditional view,"[2] this is what I mean:

> The traditional view among churches of Christ is that God Himself joins together two people in marriage and those whom God has joined together only God can disjoin. Because of this, if two people divorce, unless for the cause of adultery (fornication and adultery are used interchangeably by those who hold this view), they cannot remarry. Some also contend that if

---
[1] Scriptures quoted in this book without a version reference are taken from the King James Version (KJV).
[2] When I use this term, I do not mean to use it in a derogatory way. In fact, I myself once held this view.

a believer is abandoned by an unbeliever then he or she may marry, but not all agree on this point.

The problem with this view is that, although it is accepted doctrinally, it is not practiced in reality among some churches of Christ. In some congregations you will find couples who are considered "unscripturally divorced," and remarried, but are attending church assemblies; in these cases the issue is basically ignored. Those couples who are considered "unscripturally divorced" are often treated as second-class Christians, i.e. not fully Christians and not outsiders.

Dan Knight recognized this problem and said:

> The weakness in such an approach, of course, is that we are in essence saying, "Even though we are aware of what the Bible teaches, we can't seem to reconcile that teaching with a realistic approach to the human circumstance. Therefore, we will 'wink' at Scripture, and move on." Can this be an acceptable approach?[3]

Dr. Ken Stewart said in his book on divorce and remarriage:

> There are many churches and ministers who declare today divorce is a sin… That message was preached over and over until about half the church wound up divorced. Then, faced with the indisputable fact that, despite all the sermons and pronouncements, church members were indeed getting divorced, the preachers began declaring, "Don't remarry. It is wrong. Remarriage is a sin," until all the divorced people got remarried. Now the church doesn't know what to say… The church world has made a legalistic thing out of the whole matter of divorce, remarriage, and adultery… we've made the divorce issue so legalistic that absolutely no one could keep the laws we've established. Yet with all our legalism

---

3 Dan Knight, "What Jesus Really Said: Putting Away the Mistranslations about Divorce," article found on the academia.edu website, May 24, 2010. URL: http://www.academia.edu/3622738/What_Jesus_Really_Said_Putting_Away_the_Mistranslations_about_Divorce (accessed 7/10/17), 6.

> we still have no solution to the problem. Doesn't that tell us something about our "cure"? Basically we have just shrugged the whole thing off thinking, "well, that's another one of those things we'll understand by and by, when we all get to heaven." But we won't need the answer then. There won't be any divorce problem in heaven. We can't put it off any longer- we need answers here and now.[4]

That is my reason for writing this treatise: to supply the answers- not just any answers, but biblical answers that are practical and applicable to those who are in the midst of a marriage crisis and to those who have already experienced marriage destruction.

My concerns with the traditional view began when it became apparent to me that this view is contrary to what the bible says about grace, repentance, forgiveness, and restoration. It also appears to be contrary to everything God says about the purpose and positive value of marriage. The traditional view originally developed through the Catholic Church.[5] It was formalized into an official church doctrine at the Council of Trent in the mid-sixteenth century.[6]

This doctrine has been the predominant approach to MDR ever since. The doctrine has been tweaked and modified to varying degrees since the Protestant Reformation, but the core of the teaching is basically the same. The problem I see with the traditional teaching on MDR is its fundamental approach to the issue. The traditional view approaches MDR as a legal arrangement. The idea is that the bible speaks of marriage in legal terms; that is, marriage is basically a legal code. The typical language used in discussion of marriage is almost exclusively about what is commonly called the "marriage law." Interestingly enough, the bible never uses this term; it is nowhere found in scripture. I believe this is a wrong approach to

---

[4] Ken Stewart, DIVORCE and REMARRIAGE, (Tulsa: Harrison House, Inc., 1984), 12, 14.
[5] When the term "Catholic Church" (CC) is used in this book, it refers to the Roman Catholic Church.
[6] See APPENDIX B for a sampling of decrees concerning marriage formulated at the Council of Trent.

marriage, and if you begin with the wrong approach, the final outcome will be just as wrong. You cannot start wrong and end right. The passages we introduced at the beginning are usually referred to as "God's original marriage law." The question I wish to propose to you is this: *Was God establishing a marriage law or was He establishing a marriage relationship?* What did God say was the reason for marriage? God said it was because "...it is not good that man should be alone..."[7] The apostle Paul tells us in Ephesians that the marriage relationship parallels our relationship with God.[8] What would you think of a person who tried to find in scripture a way to destroy our relationship with God that God would find acceptable because it could be justified by certain technicalities found in the Law? Everything God says about marriage has to do with the sanctity of the relationship. What God opposes is the destruction of the relationship. When asked "...Is it lawful for a man to put away his wife for every cause?"[9] Jesus did not even acknowledge the askers' legal wrangling. He directed them to the relationship and God's opposition to its destruction. There is no lawful way to destroy the marriage relationship. The problem lies in approaching marriage as a liturgical and religious issue, as the Pharisees did, rather than a moral issue. That is not to say God did not regulate marriage. Once sin entered the picture, marriage required regulation, but these regulations seem to have been given for the purpose of protecting individual rights and preventing injustice and mistreatment rather than for purely religious reasons. Some regulations were given in the interest of maintaining a pure blood-line (Genesis 38:8-10 and Deuteronomy 25:5-6). Although this was partly for maintaining the rights of the Israelite people, it was also important in terms of the identity of the messiah. Some regulations were given for the well-being of the people rather than for purely religious reasons (such as those that deal with incest).

It is with the "one flesh" relationship that God is the most concerned. When Jesus was asked about how one might lawfully

---

7 Genesis 2:18b.
8 See Ephesians 5:22-32.
9 Matthew 19:3b.

put away his wife, Jesus directed their attention to the one flesh relationship. This relationship is so close it is how God defines mankind. God, by divine decree, arranged for humankind to be represented by both male and female in a plural unity, i.e. "one flesh"- no longer two, but one (Genesis 1:26-27; 5:1-2).

Genesis 1:26-27 **And God said, Let us make <u>man</u> in our image, after our likeness: and let <u>them</u> have dominion over the fish of the sea, and over the fowl of the air, and over the cattle, and over all the earth, and over every creeping thing that creepeth upon the earth. So God created <u>man</u> in his own image, in the image of God created he <u>him</u>; male and female created he <u>them</u>.**[10]

Genesis 5:1-2 **This is the book of the generations of Adam. In the day that God created <u>man</u>, in the likeness of God made he <u>him</u>; Male and female created he <u>them</u>; and blessed them, and called <u>their name Adam</u>, in the day when they were created.**[11]

Genesis 5:1-2 **This is the book of the generations of Adam. In the day that God created man, he made him in God's likeness. He created them male and female, and blessed them, and called their name Adam,** ("Adam" and "Man" are spelled with the exact same consonants in Hebrew, so this can be correctly translated either way.) **in the day when they were created.** (WEB)[12]

Genesis 5:1-2 **This is the book of the genealogy of Adam. In the day that God created man, He made him in the likeness of God. He created them male and female, and blessed <u>them</u> and called them <u>Mankind</u> in the day they were created.** (NKJV)[13]

---

10 Underlining added for emphasis.
11 Ibid.
12 For more information about the Bible versions used in this book, please see the Bible Version section after the bibliography. Many of the versions used in this book were accessed electronically using Power BibleCD software: Brandon Staggs, Power BibleCD, (Bronson, MI: Phil Lindner, Online Publishing, Inc., 2015). The citation for Power BibleCD is also listed in the bibliography.
13 Underlining added for emphasis.

This unity between a man and a woman is to be established in a marriage covenant. We were not created to be like the animals, but rather we were created in the image of God. As God is one in the Father, Son, and Holy Spirit, man is one in male and female as the one flesh relationship aptly expresses and the sexual act symbolizes.

I say this in order to say it is the destruction of the "one flesh" relationship that God is against, not marriage. Marriage-breaking, not marriage-making, is what God is opposed to. The attitude among some seems to be one of tolerance for marriage-breaking, provided subsequent marriage is prohibited.

Let us study this important subject together. Some of what you have always thought about MDR may be challenged in this treatise. If you resist the temptation to bail out when your thinking on the matter is challenged and stay with me to the end, I think you will find it was worth your time. I simply ask that you be like the fair-minded Bereans and give me a hearing on this matter and then search the scriptures to see if they are so.

CHAPTER I: GOD'S VIEW OF MARRIAGE

One of the most basic truths of the bible is the fact that God is *for* marriage and *against* marriage-breaking. However, with Satan, just the opposite is true on both accounts. Notice this passage in 1 Timothy 4:1-3 **Now the Spirit expressly says that in latter times some will depart from the faith, giving heed to deceiving spirits and <u>doctrines of demons</u>, speaking lies in hypocrisy, having their own conscience seared with a hot iron, <u>forbidding to marry</u>, and commanding to abstain from foods which God created to be received with thanksgiving by those who believe and know the truth.** (NKJV)[14] Paul says forbidding to marry is one of the doctrines of demons. The scripture cannot make it any plainer for us; Satan is opposed to marriage.

Let us now look at what God says about marriage and I think we will be able to see clearly why God is for marriage and Satan is opposed to marriage.

Genesis 2:18 **And the LORD God said, It is not good that the man should be alone; I will make him an help meet for him.** Has this truth changed? For those who need marriage Satan wants to change what is good, i.e. marriage, to that which is not good.

Proverbs 18:22 **Whoso findeth a wife findeth a good thing, and obtaineth favour of the LORD.** God is pleased with those who marry, and he who marries finds favor from God. On the other hand, Satan desires those who want to marry to be forbidden to marry.

1 Corinthians 7:2-9 **Nevertheless, to avoid fornication, let every man have his own wife, and let every woman have her own husband. Let the husband render unto the wife due benevolence: and likewise also the wife unto the husband. The wife hath not power of her own body, but the**

---
14 Underlining added for emphasis.

husband: and likewise also the husband hath not power of his own body, but the wife. Defraud ye not one the other, except it be with consent for a time, that ye may give yourselves to fasting and prayer; and come together again, that Satan tempt you not for your incontinency. But I speak this by permission, and not of commandment. For I would that all men were even as I myself. But every man hath his proper gift of God, one after this manner, and another after that. I say therefore to the unmarried and widows, It is good for them if they abide even as I. But if they cannot contain, let them marry: for it is better to marry than to burn. One of the vital roles of marriage in God's plan is the role marriage plays in maintaining moral purity. Olan Hicks points out "many men who are not capable of being faithful to a vow of celibacy are capable of being faithful to the vows of marriage."[15] Sex is only permitted within the parameters of marriage. Sex outside marriage is sin, so where does Satan want those who "cannot contain" or cannot exercise "self-control"[16] in this area? God says let them marry. If a man or woman is forbidden to marry, he or she is deprived of the only legitimate provision for sexual outlet. Jesus said some do not need marriage; He said some are eunuchs for various reasons (e.g. the apostle Paul), but He goes on to say not all are capable of a life of celibacy (Matthew 19:1-12). Notice: (1 Corinthians 10:13) **There hath no temptation taken you but such as is common to man: but God is faithful, who will not suffer you to be tempted above that ye are able; but will with the temptation also make a way to escape, that ye may be able to bear it.** What is God's way of escape for the temptation to commit fornication? It is marriage, of course. Some may suggest other ways to avoid fornication, but they are not biblical ways. God has given in His word the method by which fornication can be avoided. It is a fact of life that while a few can remain pure without a sexual outlet, and some even prefer it that way, most cannot. This is not to say it would be physically impossible, but the fact Paul said **if they cannot contain, let**

---

15 Olan Hicks, WHAT THE BIBLE SAYS ABOUT MARRIAGE, DIVORCE, & REMARRIAGE, (Joplin, MO: College Press Publishing Company, 1987), 13.
16 As the New King James Version (NKJV) renders the term.

them marry indicates celibacy for some would require abnormal restraint. Why look for another way of escaping fornication than the one provided by God? God says it is better to marry than to burn with passion. Satan prefers you to burn with passion. Satan is the great tempter. Olan Hicks writes:

> Christianity does not require one to be married who does not want to be. But it does condemn all sexual activity outside of marriage. Therefore one must either be married or omit all sexual activity from his life. If he cannot do the latter then the scriptures explicitly state that he must be allowed to do the former. It is a matter of simple physical reality. This is not changed by the fact that one has committed the sin of marriage breaking or of dishonoring his vows, or has had the misfortune to be married to a mate who did that to him. It is a sin to do such things but that does not change the fact of the vital nature of the right fulfillment of these needs nor does it change the fact that they can be rightly served only in marriage.[17]

In Matthew 19:10-12 the passage reads: **His disciples say unto him, If the case of the man be so with his wife, it is not good to marry. But he said unto them, All men cannot receive this saying, save they to whom it is given. For there are some eunuchs, which were so born from their mother's womb: and there are some eunuchs, which were made eunuchs of men: and there be eunuchs, which have made themselves eunuchs for the kingdom of heaven's sake. He that is able to receive it, let him receive it.** When Jesus' disciples said "it is better not to marry," Jesus immediately corrected that idea by saying that for some that is possible but for others it is not. An important observation is in the fact that Jesus did not say there are some that must be eunuchs for the Kingdom of Heaven's sake but that they make themselves eunuchs. In other words, the decision to be a eunuch was com-

---

17 Olan Hicks, DIVORCE REPENTANCE AND THE GOSPEL OF CHRIST / DIVORCE & REMARRIAGE The Issues Made Clear, (Searcy, AR: Gospel Enterprises, 1997), 33-34 of DIVORCE & REMARRIAGE The Issues Made Clear.

pletely voluntary. However, for most, marriage is very necessary in maintaining moral purity and was given by God for the benefit of man. Jesus was not requiring anyone to become a eunuch. This was meant to apply only to those who are able to receive it. Should we be trying to make eunuchs of those who are not able to receive it? (1 Corinthians 7:8-9) **I say therefore to the unmarried and widows, It is good for them if they abide even as I. But if they cannot contain, let them marry: for it is better to marry than to burn.**[18] The "unmarried" would include those never married, but it would also include those divorced. Otherwise, Paul could have simply said "to the never married and widows." Marriage is not a sin, whereas forbidding marriage is a doctrine of demons.

1 Corinthians 7:26-28 **I suppose therefore that this is good for the present distress, I say, that it is good for a man so to be. Art thou bound unto a wife? seek not to be loosed. Art thou loosed from a wife? seek not a wife. But and if thou marry, thou hast not sinned; and if a virgin marry, she hath not sinned. Nevertheless such shall have trouble in the flesh: but I spare you.** "Bound unto a wife" is referring to the marriage bond and "loosed from a wife" means divorced from a wife. The opposite of "bound" is "loosed." To be "bound to a wife" is to be married to her and to be "loosed" is to be divorced from her, and if a person in such a situation marries, he does not sin. If one is loosed from a wife, Satan wants him to stay that way, especially if he cannot contain. Paul says that if you are loosed from a wife, and you marry, you have not sinned.[19]

Hebrews 13:4 **Marriage is honourable in all, and the bed undefiled: but whoremongers and adulterers God will judge.**

Notice the word "honorable." Let's look at some passages where this word is found so that we might get a better understanding of its meaning.

---
18 See chapter 9 for a further explanation of this passage and the word "unmarried."
19 See chapter nine for further discussion of these verses.

Romans 2:7 **To them who by patient continuance in well doing seek for glory and honour and immortality, eternal life:**

Romans 2:10 **But glory, honour, and peace, to every man that worketh good, to the Jew first, and also to the Gentile:**

1 Timothy 1:17 **Now unto the King eternal, immortal, invisible, the only wise God, be honour and glory for ever and ever. Amen.**

Hebrews 13:4 says: **Marriage is honorable in** (or among) **all...** Marriage is honorable according to God, but Satan would have us believe marriage is dishonorable for those who have sinned against marriage.

Finally, in 1 Timothy 4:1-4 the scripture says: **Now the Spirit speaketh expressly, that in the latter times some shall depart from the faith, giving heed to seducing spirits, and <u>doctrines of devils</u>; Speaking lies in hypocrisy; having their conscience seared with a hot iron; <u>Forbidding to marry</u>, and commanding to abstain from meats, which God hath created to be received with thanksgiving of them which believe and know the truth. For every creature of God is good, and nothing to be refused, if it be received with thanksgiving:**[20] We need to put our focus where God instructs us to put our focus. We should teach against marriage-breaking, which God hates (Malachi 2:14-16), and not marriage-making. Marriage is portrayed by God in scripture as positive and beneficial for mankind while forbidding marriage is from Satan. The consequences of forbidding marriage are far more reaching than its effect on the divorced couple. Olan Hicks explains how forbidding marriage has an adverse effect on all of society:

> It was not for sexual purposes only that they ordered that every man be allowed a wife and every woman be allowed a husband. The home and family relationship, called in scripture 'household,' is vitally important to many aspects of civilized so-

---

20 Underlining added for emphasis.

ciety. When homes are lost and marriage is repudiated much more is lost than just the sexual outlet. Basic order and balance in life is lost to those involved and the ill effects extend in large measure to other nearby people and eventually to the whole society. The same basic considerations which in the beginning caused God to institute marriage now cry out to us and plead for retaining marriage, not just for society at large but for each individual. When in particular cases marriage gets into disrepair the answer is to repair it, not discard it. In cases where marriage has been discarded the answer is to recover it if possible. If that is not possible and a particular marriage cannot be recovered, the Bible answer still is not rejection of marriage itself. That is never the answer to anything except in those rare cases where the person is immune to the needs normally supplied by marriage.[21]

---

[21] Hicks, WHAT THE BIBLE SAYS ABOUT MARRIAGE, DIVORCE, & REMARRIAGE, 182.

CHAPTER II: THE "ONE FLESH" RELATIONSHIP AND WHEN A MARRIAGE IS A MARRIAGE

1 Timothy 4:1, 3 **1 Now the Spirit speaketh expressly, that in the latter times some shall depart from the faith, giving heed to seducing spirits, and doctrines of devils;... 3 Forbidding to marry.**

Genesis 2:18; 21-24 **18 And the LORD God said, It is not good that the man should be alone; I will make him an help meet for him... 21 And the LORD God caused a deep sleep to fall upon Adam, and he slept: and he took one of his ribs, and closed up the flesh instead thereof; 22 And the rib, which the LORD God had taken from man, made he a woman, and brought her unto the man. 23 And Adam said, This is now bone of my bones, and flesh of my flesh: she shall be called Woman, because she was taken out of Man. 24 Therefore shall a man leave his father and his mother, and shall cleave unto his wife: and they shall be one flesh.**

God created the one flesh relationship for man in order to change a "not good" situation into something that was "very good" (Genesis 1:31). This relationship and its sanctity is at the heart of everything Jesus and Paul had to say about MDR. The key to understanding the nature of this relationship is its parallel to our relationship with Christ. Ephesians 5:25-32 **Husbands, love your wives, even as Christ also loved the church, and gave himself for it; That he might sanctify and cleanse it with the washing of water by the word, That he might present it to himself a glorious church, not having spot, or wrinkle, or any such thing; but that it should be holy and without blemish. So ought men to love their wives as their own bodies. He that loveth his wife loveth himself. For no man ever yet hated his own flesh; but nourisheth and cherisheth it, even as the Lord the church: For we are members of his body, of his flesh, and of his bones. For this** cause shall a man leave his father and mother, and shall be joined unto his wife, and they two shall be one flesh. This is a great mystery: but I speak concerning Christ and the church.** This is not a marriage law, but rather the way God has designed humans to relate to one another. This is a God-designed relationship. When Jesus was asked "...Is it lawful for a man to put away his wife for every cause?,"[22] Jesus directed them back to this God-ordained one flesh relationship. His point was that one cannot lawfully put away his wife or break the one flesh relationship for any cause. What would we say to someone who asked "is it lawful for a man to put away his savior, Jesus Christ, for every cause?" There is no cause by which a man may break the one flesh relationship lawfully. Jesus said in Matthew 19:6: **Wherefore they are no more twain, but one flesh. What therefore God hath joined together, let not man put asunder.** Here is the bottom line- it is sin to break the one flesh relationship. This relationship is ordained of God to be confirmed and practiced within the marriage bond. However "put asunder" is what Jesus said man is not to do. He was not referring to the legal divorce process, but rather to the repudiating of one's spouse, the breaking of the commitments, and the discarding of the one flesh relationship. One may commit the sin of rejecting the marriage relationship without getting a divorce decree. This distinction is at the heart of much of the misunderstanding of the MDR issue.

WHEN IS A MARRIAGE A MARRIAGE?

Hebrews 13:4 **Marriage is honourable in all, and the bed undefiled: but whoremongers and adulterers God will judge.** In this verse we see certain needs that may only be met within the marriage bond. Whenever one seeks to meet those needs outside the marriage bond, he or she sins. The only lawful place where these needs may be met are within the marriage bond. The battle-line between God and Satan seems to be marital faithfulness verses illicit sex. For this reason we need to know when a marriage is a marriage and when is a marriage no longer a marriage.

---
22 Matthew 19:3b.

The main point of demarcation is the vow or covenant between a man and a woman. Genesis 2:23 **And Adam said, This is now bone of my bones, and flesh of my flesh:...** This vow is similar to our vow or covenant which we make with Christ. Ephesians 5:28-31 **So ought men to love their wives as their own bodies. He that loveth his wife loveth himself. For no man ever yet hated his own flesh; but nourisheth and cherisheth it, even as the Lord the church: For we are members of his body, of his flesh, and of his bones. For this cause shall a man leave his father and mother, and shall be joined unto his wife, and they two shall be one flesh.**

Malachi 2:14 **Yet ye say, Wherefore? Because the LORD hath been witness between thee and the wife of thy youth, against whom thou hast dealt treacherously: yet is she thy companion, and the wife of thy covenant.** Marriage is a covenant, i.e. an exchange of solemn vows of commitment a man and a woman make to one another witnessed by God. There is not a prescribed ceremony in scripture, nor does the bible tell us where or by whom it is to be performed. A man and woman can make a binding commitment before a justice of the peace or have a $40,000 ceremony, and the difference between the one and the other is about $40,000. If God had intended for the exchange of vows to be done according to a prescribed ceremony, He certainly would have given us specific instructions in this regard.

Marriage is an earthly matter: Matthew 22:23-30 **The same day came to him the Sadducees, which say that there is no resurrection, and asked him, Saying, Master, Moses said, If a man die, having no children, his brother shall marry his wife, and raise up seed unto his brother. Now there were with us seven brethren: and the first, when he had married a wife, deceased, and, having no issue, left his wife unto his brother: Likewise the second also, and the third, unto the seventh. And last of all the woman died also. Therefore in the resurrection whose wife shall she be of the seven? for they all had her. Jesus answered and said unto**

them, Ye do err, not knowing the scriptures, nor the power of God. For in the resurrection they neither marry, nor are given in marriage, but are as the angels of God in heaven. Just because marriage is an earthly matter does not mean God is not interested in how we approach and practice marriage. Money is an earthly matter, but God certainly cares how we deal with our money. God's concern with marriage, according to the scriptures, appears to be the integrity of the vow. God intends for our vows to our mate to be a permanent commitment and that both parties are absolutely faithful to that commitment. This commitment should involve a strong and deep love bond which includes a life which is fulfilling physically and intimately.

The Jews had developed certain customs in regards to marriage and the marriage ceremony. Apparently, since Jesus attended one of these ceremonies, and even participated by way of His first miracle, God accepts the procedures in regards to marriage and the marriage ceremony which are in harmony with customs and civil law, provided they are not immoral or unethical.

God does not, however, approve of man legislating on His behalf when it comes to marriage (1 Timothy 4:1-3). The Catholic Church developed a theology around marriage and turned it into a sacrament. The Catholic Church then became the sole proprietor of marriages authorized or unauthorized by God. Marriage was no longer seen as a covenant between two people and God as a witness (see Malachi 2:14). Rather (according to the Catholic Church), it became a covenant between three, the man and woman, and God.[23] The Catholic Church became the self-proclaimed arbiter for God in regards to marriage. The result of the Catholic Church and many that have been influenced by their teachings is, as Foy Wallace says: "The tendency to displace God as the judge of us all, and a preacher ascends to the bench."[24]

The Catholic Church took the statement of Jesus in Matthew

---
23 See appendix B
24 Foy Wallace, *The Sermon on the Mount and the Civil State*, (Nashville, Tennessee: Foy Wallace Publications, 1967), 41.

19:6 Wherefore they are no more twain, but one flesh. What therefore God hath joined together, let not man put asunder and changed "what therefore God hath joined together" to "<u>whom</u> God hath joined together" and "let not man put asunder" to "man <u>cannot</u> put asunder." "What" became "whom" and "let not" (or do not) became "cannot."[25] Jesus was not referring to God doing a personal joining of each couple that unites in marriage. Jesus' reference to the marriage relationship instituted in the beginning is unmistakable, and plainly establishes the context. God does not create or choose the partners in every single marriage, but He did create the one flesh relationship that all marriages through the ages were designed to be. Jesus here is looking at God's original design, not any particular marriage or marriages.

A.T. Robertson said in *Robertson's NT Word Pictures*:

> What therefore God hath joined together *(ho oun ho theos sunezeuxen)*. Note "what," not "whom." The marriage relation God has made. "The creation of sex, and the high doctrine as to the cohesion it produces between man and woman, laid down in Gen., interdict separation" (Bruce). The word for "joined together" means "yoked together," a common verb for marriage in ancient Greek. It is the timeless aorist indicative *(sunezeuxen)*, true always.[26]

What God joined together was the one flesh. It is and was and always will be the case that mankind was meant to unite

---

[25] If God had meant "<u>whom</u>" He likely would have used a masculine plural relative pronoun. The Holy Spirit used a neuter singular relative pronoun. The word is usually translated "what" when it is neuter gender in the Greek and "who" in the masculine gender, although not always. If the context demands a "who" from a neuter gender, it may be translated "who," provided the translator has made an accurate exegesis of the passage. The Greek supports "what," and the context clearly indicates "what' rather than "who."
[26] Archibald Thomas Robertson, *Word Pictures in the New Testament*, (New York: Harper & Brothers, 1930 [the version used may have been updated in 1960]), commentary for Matthew 19:6, accessed electronically via *Power BibleCD*. See the bibliography section for more information about *Power BibleCD*.

in this one flesh relationship. God approves and recognizes those who unite with one another according to His will. God does not unite them in Heaven. The man leaves father and mother and cleaves to a wife, according to God's will. They become one flesh as God has ordained (from the beginning) that all men and women should do who need to relate to one another intimately on Earth. God does not unite the individual couple in marriage any more than He chooses individuals for salvation. Those who are saved are saved according to a predestined plan and those who are united in marriage are united according to a predestined plan (Genesis 2:24). The one flesh relationship is the "what" to which Jesus was referring. When I speak of the traditional view I am referring to the notion a man cannot disjoin a man and a woman joined together in marriage. I am not claiming that someone who holds the traditional view accepts all that the Catholic Church has decreed concerning marriage. There are varying degrees to which those in the church have been influenced by the teachings of the Catholic Church. When I refer to the traditional view I am referring to the claim: "those whom God has joined together, man cannot disjoin."

When Jesus said "let not man put asunder," He was referring to the one flesh relationship rather than a legal divorce. He was saying "do not break apart what God has joined together." Whether a legal divorce takes place or not is beside the point. He does not want us to sunder the relationship. There are those who are living in the same house and because of their beliefs about divorce, have destroyed their relationship even though they have not divorced officially. They think it is the official and lawful divorce that God is opposed to and they are very much mistaken. The relationship is always broken before any legal divorce takes place and it is the relationship for which God is concerned.

It is not true to say man cannot do what God says he should not do or to say man cannot do what God has prohibited. Just as it is not true, as the Calvinists teach, that a man cannot fall from grace in spite of all the warnings in scripture about falling from grace. To prove my point, ask yourself this question: *If a husband murders his wife, has he disjoined himself from his wife?* Certainly all would have to admit the man has disjoined himself from his wife! Without God's approval, I might add.

Because certain needs may only be lawfully met within the marriage bond, we need to know what constitutes a marriage bond. We also need to know when the marriage bond is over.

What constitutes a legal official divorce? It is very simple: Deuteronomy 24:1 says: **When a man hath taken a wife, and married her, and it come to pass that she find no favour in his eyes, because he hath found some uncleanness in her: then let him write her a bill of divorcement, and give it in her hand, and send her out of his house.**

1. **[S]he find no favour in his eyes, because he hath found some uncleanness in her** (the marriage is sundered, the wife is put away) this is the destruction of the relationship, not the legal release.

2. **[T]hen let him write her a bill of divorcement, and give it in her hand** (this is referred to as a "get" in the Jewish community. Divorce papers, or a legal declaration, are written, witnessed, and signed signifying the marriage is no longer binding).

3. **[A]nd send her out of his house** (this refers to a permanent and official separation, recognized publicly by community and state.)

The marriage begins with vows of a lifelong commitment to one another and should only be broken by death. However, to say man cannot break his or her marriage is to ignore the fact that men and women have, and God recognized that they did.

Jesus said "do not," but He never said man "could not."

A major problem in understanding MDR has been the lack of understanding between the breaking of the marriage relationship and divorce. Notice God commanded divorce. Deuteronomy 24:1 **When a man hath taken a wife, and married her, and it come to pass that she find no favour in his eyes, because he hath found some uncleanness in her: then let him write her a bill of divorcement, and give it in her hand, and send her out of his house.** Mark 10:3-5 **And he answered and said unto them, What did Moses command you? And they said, Moses suffered <u>to write a bill of divorcement</u>, and to put her away. And Jesus answered and said unto them, For the hardness of your heart he wrote you this precept.**[27]

God also says He hates "putting away." Malachi 2:14-16 **Yet ye say, Wherefore? Because the LORD hath been witness between thee and the wife of thy youth, against whom thou hast dealt treacherously: yet is she thy companion, and the wife of thy covenant. And did not he make one? Yet had he the residue of the spirit. And wherefore one? That he might seek a godly seed. Therefore take heed to your spirit, and let none deal treacherously against the wife of his youth. For the LORD, the God of Israel, saith that <u>he hateth putting away</u>: for one covereth violence with his garment, saith the LORD of hosts: therefore take heed to your spirit, that ye deal not treacherously.**[28] Many of the problems that exists in regards to MDR are because of the failure to make a distinction between the divorce decree which God commanded to be given and the "putting away" which He said He hates and referred to as "treachery." The divorce decree or "writing of divorcement" does not break the marriage relationship, but rather the divorce is given because the marriage is broken. The divorce decree is similar to a death certificate. When a parent dies and you are the executor of his or her estate, you cannot settle their affairs without an official document declaring them officially dead. The death certificate is not what killed the parent; it is given because the parent is

---
27 Underlining added for emphasis.
28 Ibid.

dead. The divorce decree does not kill the marriage; it is given because the marriage is dead. There have been husbands and wives who have permanently separated, but, because of their religious beliefs about divorce, have never divorced. There have been those whose marriages are bankrupt but who do not divorce because of their children. Nevertheless, the one flesh relationship has been broken in such cases and the marriage is dead even though they live in the same house. The purpose of the divorce decree according to God in Deuteronomy 24:1-4 is to legally release the wife from the marriage bond. When the husband gives her a writing of divorcement, she is no longer legally bound to the marriage; she is free, unhitched, unmarried, and single, and she may go and be another man's wife. Observation of Deuteronomy 24:1-2 indicates God is not against the divorce when it becomes necessary. Part of the problem with our understanding of divorce is thinking in terms of what cases allows for divorce or "causes for divorce." All the talk about causes for divorce is foreign to scripture; neither Moses nor Jesus nor Paul addressed the idea of causes for divorce. We have been conditioned to think Jesus was talking about causes for divorce in Matthew chapters 5 and 19, but He was actually talking about causes for adultery. The divorce decree, or writing of divorcement, is always given for one reason, and that is because the marriage is dead. What killed the marriage is a different issue. The sin is in what killed the marriage, not in the writing of divorcement. It is what killed the marriage that God condemns, not the writing of divorcement. The writing of divorcement is a legal release from a destroyed marriage; it neither condemns nor condones what destroyed the marriage. The writing of divorcement was from the mind of God, not from man. God gave it as a remedy to the fallout of man's sinful practices. To say a woman that has been given a writing of divorcement and sent away is still bound in marriage to her former husband is contrary to common sense, the bible, and every civilized society that has ever existed. We, as Christians, must do all that is humanly possible to prevent marriages from becoming broken. Furthermore, if a marriage is already broken, we must do what we can to prevent the situation from reaching the point where the divorce decree becomes necessary. Early prevention is the key to protecting the integrity of marriage as God would have it, not demonizing those who have divorced.

The most damaging aspect of the traditional teaching is the omission of grace in correcting the sin of marriage-breaking and the confusing of atonement with restitution. It is a punitive rather than a redemptive approach to the problem. The thinking is that if a man divorces his wife and marries another, then to make things right and repent, he must break his second marriage and remarry his former wife. Usually the argument is along the lines of: if a man steals a car, to make it right he must give the car back. What the man repents of is having a heart of dishonesty which led him to stealing the car. If he repents (has a change of heart), God will forgive him and the man will stop stealing. The man would give the car back because the car does not belong to him. It would not be correct to say giving the car back would atone for his sin, nor would a vow to never again own or drive a car be atonement for his sin. The atonement for the man's sin is the sacrificial blood of Jesus. The repentance would be a change of mind about being dishonest and his atonement would be through the grace of God in Christ's sacrifice on the cross. Giving the car back might be the right thing to do, but such an act would not unsteal the car or undo the sin. This scenario does not parallel the marriage situation because when a man gives a woman the writing of divorcement and marries another, the former wife is no longer his wife, and he is now the husband of another woman. Similarly, if a man sold his car and gave the buyer a signed bill of sale, the buyer would not have to give the car back because he has a signed bill of sale showing the former owner no longer has a claim to the car. The bill of sale is similar to the bill of divorcement in that it serves much the same purpose. The very purpose of God commanding the bill of divorcement be given, in the event a man puts his wife away, is to release her legally and to sever any claim to her by her former husband. She would be free to marry another and her former husband could not claim, as some did, no divorce had taken place, which is the hardness of heart Jesus refers to in Matthew 19 and the reason God commanded the bill of divorcement be given in Deuteronomy 24. If a man, having been formerly divorced and remarried, was to divorce his second wife, he would commit the sin of marriage-breaking with the woman who is his wife. If he then tried to go back to his former wife and his former wife is remarried, he would not only have broken his covenant with his current wife, he would be trying to take a woman that is not his wife, but is somebody else's wife, and encourage her to break her covenant with the one who is her husband.[29]

What, then, is one to do in the case of having broken a marriage? The answer is in Isaiah 55:7-8: **Let the wicked forsake his way, and the unrighteous man his thoughts: and let him return unto the LORD, and he will have mercy upon him; and to our God, for he will abundantly pardon. For my thoughts are not your thoughts, neither are your ways my ways, saith the LORD.** Note the wicked is to forsake his way and return to the Lord and to His way. God's ideal is a man and a woman committed to one another for life. Man's practice is putting away wives to marry others i.e. going from mate to mate. If the wicked forsakes his way, he stops putting away wives to marry others. If he returns to God's way, he will commit to the woman he is now married to for life and God will forgive him. **For I will be merciful to their unrighteousness, and their sins and their iniquities will I remember no more** (Hebrews 8:12).

When sin occurs it means that a man is not looking at things in the same way God does. In the case of a man who breaks marriage vows repeatedly, puts away a wife to get another, and keeps repeating that process, his view of marriage is diametrically opposed to that of God's view on the matter. God has in mind a man and a woman in a life-long commitment in marriage. What needs to happen is this man needs to be taught God's way and to be shown the wrongness of going from mate to mate, and he needs to see marriage the way God sees mar-

---

[29] Because of the traditional view, many have confused repentance with restitution. Restitution is a biblical subject, but is restitution the same as repentance? For this reason I have included a short discussion of the subject of restitution and repentance in an appendix.

riage and start honoring his marriage vows. If he does, he has thus repented and is determined to honor his marriage vows from this day forward, but he can only begin now. He cannot repent yesterday, but the blood of Jesus can reach into the past. If he repents, then God will forgive him, because of the cross and a man named Jesus (2 Timothy 2:25).

One may tell a man who has been divorced and remarried to stay with the wife he is married to and to not divorce her; likewise, he may tell a woman who has been divorced and remarried to stay with the husband she is married to and to not divorce him. To accuse the one giving such advice of promoting divorce just does not make any sense to me. Does it make sense to you? If one steals something, he cannot un-steal it. If he tells a lie, he cannot un-tell it. If he breaks his marriage vows, he cannot un-break them. What he can do is repent and stop stealing, stop lying, and stop breaking his marriage vows. He can seek God's forgiveness for stealing, lying, or breaking marriage vows, and God will forgive these sins as He does all others.

CHAPTER III: ADULTERY, FORNICATION, AND "PUTTING AWAY"

1 Timothy 4:1,3a **Now the Spirit speaketh expressly, that in the latter times some shall depart from the faith, giving heed to seducing spirits, and doctrines of devils;... 3 Forbidding to marry...**

Genesis 2:18; 20-24 **18 And the LORD God said, It is not good that the man should be alone; I will make him an help meet for him.... 21 And the LORD God caused a deep sleep to fall upon Adam, and he slept: and he took one of his ribs, and closed up the flesh instead thereof; 22 And the rib, which the LORD God had taken from man, made he a woman, and brought her unto the man. 23 And Adam said, This is now bone of my bones, and flesh of my flesh: she shall be called Woman, because she was taken out of Man. 24 Therefore shall a man leave his father and his mother, and shall cleave unto his wife: and they shall be one flesh.**

The Catholic Church developed a theology around MDR, and because the bible for a time was withheld from the common people (for the most part), men and women were at the mercy of the Catholic clergy pertaining to MDR. When the bible began to be available to the common people and certain men began to question the teachings of the Catholic Church, the Protestant Reformation began. The Reformation was a good step in the right direction, but certain individuals came along and realized trying to reform such a corrupted system was not going to accomplish the goal to teach only God's word. The Restoration Movement began and the goal was to go back to the source, i.e., the word of God, alone for one's faith and practice. This was a noble goal to which many are still committed today. Many of the early restorationists rejected the sacrament view of the Catholic Church, however, some held on to some of the traditional roots pertaining to MDR, and these traditions are still among us. Some words and phrases that are used today have developed meanings through these traditions and are commonly accepted by man. Our goal should be to go to the bible and let the bible be the final word as to what a word or phrase means, as well as the truth of the matter as it pertains to MDR. We are going to look at some words and phrases and see if we can determine what they mean by how they are used in scripture. Many will point to lexicons and bible dictionaries in support of the traditional view. We need to understand lexicographers do not always define a word correctly because of some modern influence (i.e. post apostolic). For example, some define the word "baptize" to include sprinkling or pouring. However, as we observe the word as it is used in scripture, we see the word "baptize" always refers to a burial and never to sprinkling or pouring; therefore, we reject the lexicographer's definition. The bible is not a dictionary, per se, but by examining how a word is used in scripture, it will define the word for us. <u>A word should always be understood in harmony with all its uses in scripture</u>; that is the restoration plea.

Thayer himself says in the preface of his lexicon:

> The lexicographer often cannot assign a particular New Testament reference to one or another of the acknowledged significations of a word without <u>his exposition</u> of the passage in which the reference occurs. In such a case he is compelled to assume, at least to some extent, the functions of the exegete.[30]

A.T. Robertson says:

> After all is done, instances remain where syntax cannot say the last word, where theological bias will inevitably determine how one interprets the Greek idiom. .... So in Acts 2:38 εις does not of itself express design (see Mt. 10:41), but it may be so used. When the grammarian has finished, the theologian steps in, and sometimes before the grammarian is through.[31]

---
30 Joseph Henry Thayer, *GREEK-ENGLISH LEXICON of the NEW TESTAMENT* (Grand Rapids, Michigan: Baker Book House, 1977), 13. Underlining added for emphasis.
31 A.T. Robertson, *A GRAMMAR OF THE GREEK NEW TESTAMENT IN THE LIGHT OF HISTORICAL RESEARCH* (Nashville, Tennessee: Broadman Press, 1934), 389.

We need to keep in mind that most, if not all, modern day lexicographers have the traditional predilection to MDR. Our goal through this study is to let the bible be the final arbiter as to what a word or phrase means or refers. The bible always trumps the lexicons for, IT IS NOT *WHO* IS RIGHT THAT MATTERS, BUT *WHAT* IS RIGHT.

THE MEANING OF ADULTERY:

The Greek word translated "adultery" is *moichao* and the Hebrew word is *naaph*.

Most authorities define adultery as a sex act involving a married person with someone who is not their spouse. If you take a concordance and look up the word "adultery," you will find the word is used in reference to many things other than sexual activity.

Matthew 12:39 **But he answered and said unto them, An evil and adulterous generation seeketh after a sign; and there shall no sign be given to it, but the sign of the prophet Jonas:** Here adultery is said to be equal to seeking after a sign; obviously, this is not a reference to sexual activity.

James 4:4 **Ye adulterers and adulteresses, know ye not that the friendship of the world is enmity with God? whosoever therefore will be a friend of the world is the enemy of God.** Once again we have a passage that equates something other than sexual activity to the word "adultery," i.e. "friendship of the world."

Jeremiah 3:9 **And it came to pass through the lightness of her whoredom, that she defiled the land, and committed adultery with stones and with stocks.** Here we have adultery committed with "stones" and "stocks." Obviously this is not a reference to sexual activity. Some claim in this passage that spiritual adultery is committed. This is said in an attempt to diminish, if not to dismiss, the teaching in the Bible that adultery can be committed in ways other than through a sex act. This passage plainly teaches that the adultery is really, actually, and truly committed with stones and stocks, not through a sex act. In this context verse 14 tells us marital adultery is in view. **Turn, O backsliding children, saith the LORD; for I am married unto you:...**[32]

In Hosea 7:1-3, God says the people of Israel did many ungodly things, none of which were sexual, but in verse four He says: "they are all adulterers."

Thayer cites Revelation 2:22 as a case in which a form of this word refers to those who "are drawn away to idolatry." He also gives as a meaning "to falsify, to corrupt." He also gives as one of its meanings "to usurp unlawful control over the sea."[33] There are a variety of different acts which the bible says constitutes adultery (idolatry, unfaithfulness, worldliness, and even seeking after a sign), but one ingredient is common to them all, betrayal to one's vows or covenant.

In the marriage passages in Matthew, Mark, and Luke, Jesus applies adultery to two acts, putting away one's wife, and marrying another. No other acts or actions are mentioned as being adultery. Those who say the adultery is committed by the sexual acts in the subsequent marriage relationship are reading into the word of God. As bible students, we should accept the texts just as they are stated and refrain from reading the text through our preconceptions. Why not accept the text as is without addition? The reason is the text as written needs help to fit the traditional view. Later, when we look into the specifics of Jesus' statements, we will see that according to the Greek construction of the passages, the putting away and marrying another are to be viewed as contemporaneous in time with the leading verb "adultery." That is, they are viewed as happening simultaneously or at the same time.

Matthew 5:28 **But I say unto you, That whosoever looketh on a woman to lust after her hath committed adultery with**

---

32 Jeremiah 3:14a.
33 Joseph H. Thayer, *THAYER'S GREEK-ENGLISH LEXICON OF THE NEW TESTAMENT: Coded to Strong's Numbering System*, (Peabody, Massachusetts: Hendrickson Publishers, Inc., 2009), 417.

her already in his heart. In this passage no physical sex act is committed, but rather a sex thought. This shows us the legal technicalities are not those with which the Lord is most concerned. Rather, His focus is on the attitude of the man's heart as it relates to his commitment to his mate. This passage points clearly to this being primarily a moral issue as opposed to a legal one. The intent of the heart is God's focus in the law and this is what Jesus is trying to stress to these legalistic Jews. Jesus is not presenting this as a minor infraction- He says it is adultery and it is to be understood as the sin of adultery. The man sins against the marriage vows in his heart which is not a slight infraction but a serious matter. The seriousness of this mindset is often overlooked and ignored because the sin of adultery is only seen traditionally as a sex act. There is no such thing as mindless adultery, but there is adultery that does not involve the physical sex act.

I believe the original meaning of the word translated "adultery" has been altered and is now being defined in a way that changes the focus of the marriage passages containing this word from a sin of marriage-breaking to a sin of marriage-making.

Notice how the Greek word was translated into English by the earliest translations:[34]

Wycliffe Bible 1385[35]

Mt 19:9 **Trewly I seie to 3ou that who euer leeueth his wif, no but for fornicacioun, and weddith an other, doth a vowtrie; and he that weddith the forsaken wife, doth a vowtrie.** Wycliffe used the word "avowtrie" which is built on the word "vow" with the "a" in front making it a negative similar to the word "atheist." The word "avowtrie" carries the idea that the man who sends away his wife and takes another does something against the vow or marriage covenant.

---

34 Underlining for passages in this section was added for emphasis.
35 This copy of this passage from John Wycliffe's translation was quoted from *BOTP: The Early English Language Bible Reading Library*, URL: www.bibleofthepast.com/texts/file1540.htm. Unfortunately this site has changed and early translations are no longer available to read on this site.

Tyndale Bible 1526[36]

Mt 19:9 **I saye therfore vnto you whosoever putteth awaye his wyfe (except it be for fornicacion) and maryeth another breaketh wedlocke**. And whosoever maryeth her which is divorsed doeth commyt **advoutry**.

Coverdale Bible 1535[37]

Matthew 19:9 **But I saye vnto you: Whosoeuer putteth awaye his wife (excepte it be for fornicacion) and marieth another, breaketh wedlocke**. And who so marieth her yt is deuorced, commytteth **aduoutrye**.

Great Bible, 1540[38]

Matthew 19:9 **I saye vnto you: whosoeuer putteth awaye his wyfe (except it be for fornicacion) & marieth another breaketh wedlocke**. And whoso marieth her whych is deuorsed, doeth commyt **aduoutry**.

Matthew Bible-Becke; 1549[39]

Matthew 19:9 **I say therfore vnto you, whosoeuer putteth awaye hys wyfe (except it be for fornicacion) & marieth another, breaketh wedloke**. And whosoeuer maryeth her which is diuorced doth commit **aduoutry**.

I believe these early translators captured the true meaning of *moichos* in these passages.

Notice these translations of Ezekiel 16:38 and how they translate the Hebrew word *naaph*, the word translated "adultery" in

---

[36] This copy of this passage from William Tyndale's 1526 translation was accessed on the website of Northwest Nazarene University in the *Wesley Center Online* section. The website acknowledges the help of Ron Bailey in making the file available. URL: http://wesley.nnu.edu/fileadmin/imported_site/tyndale/mat.txt (accessed 2/9/17).
[37] This copy of this passage from Myles Coverdale's 1535 translation was accessed on the bibles-online.net website which lists a copyright notice of 2010. URL: http://www.bibles-online.net/1535/NewTestament/1-Matthew/ (accessed 2/9/17).
[38] This copy of this passage from the Great Bible was accessed on the originalbibles.com website. URL: https://www.originalbibles.com/Zip/Zippy.php?../SpecialBibles/Zip1/GreatBible1540.zip?GreatBible1540_Part219.pdf (accessed 2/9/17). The "&" sign was substituted for the "and" sign used in the original text. The website lists a copyright notice from 2012-2015.
[39] This copy of this passage from Edmund Becke's 1549 edition of the Matthew Bible was quoted from BOTP: The Early English Language Bible Reading Library, URL: www.bibleofthepast.com/texts/file1540.htm. Unfortunately this site has changed and the early Bible editions are no longer available from this site.

the Old Testament.[40]

And I will judge thee, as women that <u>break wedlock</u> and shed blood are judged; and I will give thee blood in fury and jealousy. (KJV)

And I will judge thee, as women that <u>break wedlock</u> and shed blood are judged; and I will bring upon thee the blood of wrath and jealousy. (ASV)

And you will be judged by me as women are judged who have been <u>untrue to their husbands</u> and have taken life; and I will let loose against you passion and bitter feeling. (BBE)

"And I will judge you as women who <u>break wedlock</u> or shed blood are judged; I will bring blood upon you in fury and jealousy. (NKJV)

And I will judge you as women who <u>break wedlock</u> and shed blood are judged, and bring upon you the blood of wrath and jealousy. (RSV)

I will judge you, as women who <u>break wedlock</u> and shed blood are judged; and I will bring on you the blood of wrath and jealousy. (WEB)

I will find you guilty of being an <u>unfaithful wife</u> and a murderer, and in my fierce anger I will sentence you to death! (CEV [Contemporary English Version])

Did you know the English word "adultery" did not exist before the middle of the 16th century? In 385 A.D. Jerome translated the Greek text into Latin. In this version he translated the Greek word *moichao* into the Latin word *adulterium* which means "...blending/mixing of different strains/ingredients; contamination."[41] This makes the passage say the man who puts away

---

[40] Underlining in the passages in this section was added for emphasis. For more information about the Bible versions, please see the Bible version information listed after the bibliography.
[41] JM Latin-English Dictionary, s.v. "adulterium." John Madsen, creator, URL: http://dictionary.babylon-software.com/adulterium/ (accessed 2/9/17).

his wife and marries another alters his marriage covenant i.e. he adulterates the marriage. This word did not make a reference to a sinful physical act, rather the reference was to what was being done to the marriage being broken. In 1560 A.D. a group of reformers while in exile at Geneva made a translation of the bible called the Geneva Bible. The Geneva translators adopted the Latin word *adulterium* for the Greek word *moichao* and by dropping the ending and adding "ie" they formed a new word, *adulterie*. In 1568 another translation was made predominantly by Bishops in the Catholic Church which was called the Bishops Bible. The Bishops dropped the "ie" of the Geneva Bible and inserted a "y" and again a new word was formed "adultery." The word took on a meaning much different than the original Greek word *moichao*. In 1611 the original King James Bible was published and the word "adultery" was retained from the Bishops Bible, and most (if not all) English translations have followed suit.

> Thus the Latin word *adulterio* worked its way into Roman translations through Jerome in the divorce passages and the English word 'adultery' came into English versions through reliance by some translators upon Latin precedents. The idea fits so perfectly with the Catholic 'sacrament' concept of marriage, which during the same time period came to be established around the world, that a majority of modern scholars have evidently accepted the whole package and have not thought to re-examine it from a more objective standpoint... It was a new word introduced into the English text and it eventually evolved and brought about a serious revision in the sense of the passages where it occurs. Primarily what has been lost in this revision is the basic idea of sinning against marriage by breaking it. The idea of betrayal of vows, or covenant obligations, has been replaced with the idea of a sinful sexual practice in the subsequent marriage relationship.[42]

Foy Wallace says:

---

[42] Hicks, *WHAT THE BIBLE SAYS ABOUT MARRIAGE, DIVORCE, & REMARRIAGE*, 154, 155.

The word 'adultery' in New Testament usage does not necessarily refer to the sinful physical act, it is not restricted to the one way of violating the bond. In the four passages in Matthew, Mark, and Luke the term adultery is given the sense of ignoring the bond.[43]

Mark 10:11 And he saith unto them, Whosoever shall put away his wife, and marry another, committeth adultery against her. In this passage the adultery is said to be committed against his first wife, not with the second wife. This scripture contradicts the traditional view that the adultery is committed with the second wife. Rather, the marrying of the second wife is only wrong in the sense it is seen as involved in the breaking of the previous marriage covenant. Jesus says it is wrong to forsake/abandon, i.e., swap, one wife for another. The putting away of one wife for another or "wife swapping" breaks one's vow with his first wife. The adultery said to be committed in this passage is obviously not referring to the sexual physical act since the relationship between the husband and first wife (concerning whom the adultery is committed) has been broken.

Malachi 2:14-16 Yet ye say, Wherefore? Because the LORD hath been witness between thee and the wife of thy youth, against whom thou hast dealt treacherously: yet is she thy companion, and the wife of thy covenant. And did not he make one? Yet had he the residue of the spirit. And wherefore one? That he might seek a godly seed. Therefore take heed to your spirit, and let none deal treacherously against the wife of his youth. For the LORD, the God of Israel, saith that he hateth putting away: for one covereth violence with his garment, saith the LORD of hosts: therefore take heed to your spirit, that ye deal not treacherously. God makes it clear in this passage that it is the putting away of one's wife and the breaking of the marriage vows that offends Him; He calls it treachery.

---

[43] Foy Wallace, *The Sermon on the Mount and the Civil State*, (Nashville, Tennessee: Foy Wallace Publications, 1967), 42.

John 8:3-4 And the scribes and Pharisees brought unto him a woman taken in adultery; and when they had set her in the midst, They say unto him, Master, this woman was taken in adultery, in the very act. "Aha," (you say), "this verse is certainly speaking of the sexual act!" Certainly sexual activity is implied (although not explicitly stated) by this verse, but was the act adultery because it was sexual or because it was an act of unfaithfulness to the marriage covenant? For example, an apple is a fruit, but that does not mean the definition of fruit is "apple." An apple is a type of fruit, but not the only type of fruit. Just as the physical act may be a type of adultery, it is not the only type of adultery; seeking after a sign is a type of adultery, idolatry is another, and putting away a wife and marrying another is also a type of adultery.

What about the word "fornication"? Are the words "fornication" and "adultery" synonyms? The word "fornication" is from the Greek word *porneia* in the NT and the Hebrew word *zanah* in the OT. The basic meaning of the word is to commit prostitution or prostitute oneself, in the verb form, or to be identified as a prostitute in the noun form. It also has a broader meaning, according to how it is used in scripture, to include unlawful intimate unions. This word is translated "fornication," "playing the harlot," "whoring," "whoredoms," "whoremonger," and related terms. This sin refers to prostitution (Deuteronomy 23:18), incest (1 Corinthians 5:1), premarital sex (Deuteronomy 22:13-21), extramarital sex (Deuteronomy 22:13-21), homosexuality (Jude 7), and idolatry (Ezekiel 16:15-17; 26).

Fornication and adultery are not synonyms- they are not to be used interchangeably. Notice the following passages.

Matthew 15:19 For out of the heart proceed evil thoughts, murders, adulteries, fornications, thefts, false witness, blasphemies:

Mark 7:21 For from within, out of the heart of men, proceed evil thoughts, adulteries, fornications, murders,

1 Corinthians 6:9 **Know ye not that the unrighteous shall not inherit the kingdom of God? Be not deceived: neither fornicators, nor idolaters, nor adulterers, nor effeminate, nor abusers of themselves with mankind,**

Galatians 5:19 **Now the works of the flesh are manifest, which are these; Adultery, fornication, uncleanness, lasciviousness,**

<u>In Hebrews 13:4, a clear and definite distinction is made between fornication and adultery.</u>

Hebrews 13:4 4 **Let marriage be had in honor among all, and let the bed be undefiled: for fornicators and adulterers God will judge.** (ASV) By substituting "adulterers" for "fornicators" in this passage, we can easily see that the words are different in meaning.

Hebrews 13:4 4 **Let marriage be had in honor among all, and let the bed be undefiled: for [adulterers] and adulterers God will judge.** (ASV)[44] Does that make sense to you?

Included in the Greek Septuagint translation of the Old Testament are a collection of books called the apocrypha. These are not inspired books, but since Jesus quoted the Septuagint more often than from the Hebrew text, He would have been familiar with the apocrypha, as would the apostles. There is a passage in the apocrypha that will give us some insight as to how Jesus and the apostles of the first century would have understood fornication and adultery. Sirach 23:22-23 "so it is with a woman who leaves her husband; and provides an heir by a stranger. 23 For first of all, she has disobeyed the law of the Most High; second, she has committed offense against her husband; and third, she has committed adultery <u>through harlotry</u> and brought forth children by another man." (NRSV)[45] The word "harlotry" in this passage is the Greek word *porneia* in the Septuagint. This quote shows the adultery is committed by means of fornication. One last point of interest: the Septua-

---
44 With the word "fornicators" changed to "adulterers."
45 Underlining has been added for emphasis.

gint never translates the Hebrew word for adultery (i.e. *naaph*) using the Greek word *porneia*!

One objection to adultery being an act committed in putting away and marrying another, rather than subsequent sex in the second marriage, is based on Greek grammar. The objection is based on the claim that the present tense of a verb always denotes a continuing action (as in "committeth adultery"), and the use of "eth" ending in the King James Version reveals in English this meaning. Following are some of the statements made by certain scholars in regards to this issue. These scholars are considered experts in the field of New Testament Greek. I am not presenting them as the last word on the subject, realizing these people are not infallible. Rather, I present them for consideration as their statements support my position on the marriage and divorce question, and because they are recognized Greek scholars. For those who have little or no knowledge of Greek, the following passages of scripture were deliberately chosen as examples because the tense of the verbs in these passages are easily discernible in English without any knowledge of Greek. Therefore, whether you are familiar with the Greek or not familiar with the Greek, hopefully you will find this portion of our study interesting and informative.

Concerning the "eth" ending, Dr. Carroll Osburn, a former professor of Greek at Abilene Christian University, calls the notion the "eth" ending in the KJV means a continuing action a "syntactical monstrosit[y]."[46]

Consider what A.T. Robertson says in regards to grammatical vices related to English translations and Greek tenses:

> It is the commonest grammatical vice for one to make a conjectural translation into English and then to discuss the syntactical propriety of the Greek tense on the basis of this translation.[47]

---
[46] Carroll D. Osburn, "Interpreting Greek Syntax," in *Biblical Interpretation: Principles and Practice: Studies in Honor of Jack Pearl Lewis, Professor of Bible, Harding Graduate School of Religion*, Edited by F. Furman, Kearley, Edward P. Myers, and Timothy D. Hadley, (Grand Rapids, MI: Baker Book House, 1986), 234.
[47] Robertson, *A Grammar of the Greek New Testament*, 821.

The following are samplings of passages having words with the "eth" ending that are point action, not continuous.[48]

J.W. Roberts says:

> The action implied in an aorist may actually have been continuous, repeated, interrupted, etc. But the aorist treats the action as a point, simply as having taken place. ἔζησεν, he lived.[49]

James 5:20 **Let him know, that he which converteth** (*epistrepsas* First aorist active articular participle of *epistrephô*; the aorist tense is always viewed as point action) **the sinner from the error of his way shall save a soul from death, and shall hide a multitude of sins.**

Leviticus 24:17 **And he that killeth** (in the LXX *pataxe* aorist active i.e. point action) **any man shall surely be put to death.**

John 16:2 **They shall put you out of the synagogues: yea, the time cometh, that whosoever killeth** (*apokteinas* aorist tense i.e. point action) **you will think that he doeth God service.**

James 1:11 **For the sun is no sooner risen with a burning heat, but it withereth** (aorist tense i.e. point action) **the grass and the flower thereof falleth** (aorist tense i.e. point action)**, and the grace of the fashion of it perisheth:** (aorist tense) **so also shall the rich man fade away in his ways.** The grass does not keep on withering, the flower does not keep on falling, and the grace does not keep on perishing.

The verbs in these passages are all aorist tense. The Greek aorist tense is always viewed as point action.[50] The scholars who translated the KJV were trained in both the NT Greek and

---

48 Underlining and information about the Greek grammar in these Biblical passages have been added for emphasis and/or information.
49 J.W. Roberts, *A GRAMMAR OF THE GREEK NEW TESTAMENT FOR BEGINNERS*, edited by Donald L. Potter, accessed electronically on the *donpotter.net* website URL: http://www.donpotter.net/pdf/roberts_grammar.pdf (accessed 2/9/17), 2014, page number 85 of pdf, listed as page 65 in text. Underlining added for emphasis.
50 The action of the aorist tense is viewed as point action, but it is not necessarily viewing an action as taking place in a moment or instant in time. It can be viewing an action in its totality, for example in Acts 26:5 "I lived a pharisee." In Greek the verb denotes kind of action

the King's English. If the "eth" ending meant linear action in English, it is unlikely the translators would have made such an elementary mistake as to translate verbs in the Greek aorist tense into English with the "eth" ending.

The present tense verb does not always denote continuing action, as goes the claim of those who take the traditional view. The mood of the verb must be considered in determining what kind of action is in view. In the *present imperative* mood, the verb is almost always a continuing action. For example, passages such as Matthew 6:33 **But seek ye first the kingdom of God, and his righteousness; and all these things shall be added unto you.** (i.e. keep on seeking [underlining added]) and Colossians 3:1 **If ye then be risen with Christ, seek those things which are above, where Christ sitteth on the right hand of God,** are in the present tense, *imperative* mood. It is unfortunate that many who hold to the traditional view will quote the above passages in an attempt to establish "committeth adultery" in Matthew 19:9 as continuing action. However, the verb in Matthew 19:9 is in the present tense *indicative* mood. The failure to distinguish between the present tenses in the imperative and indicative mood, whether out of ignorance or deliberately, is the cause of much confusion in the MDR debate.

Dana and Mantey:

> This is not, however, its excusive significance. It is a mistake to suppose that a durative meaning monopolizes the present stem.[51]

J Gresham Machen:

> In the present tense, there is in Greek no distinction between I loose, which simply represents the action as taking place in present time, and I am loosing, which calls attention to the continuance of the action.[52]

---

[51] H. E. Dana & Julius R. Mantey, *A MANUAL GRAMMAR OF THE GREEK NEW TESTAMENT*, (Toronto, Ontario: The Macmillan Co., 1955), 181.
[52] J Gresham Machen, *NEW TESTAMENT GREEK FOR BEGINNERS*, (Toronto, Ontario:

H.P.V. Nunn:

> The Present tense is occasionally used in an Aoristic sense to denote a simple event in present time, without any thought of action in progress... In these cases the context alone can decide whether the Greek Present is to be translated by the English Present Continuous or Present Simple.[53]

Concerning present tense *indicative* mood A.T. Robertson says:

> This defect is chiefly found in the indicative, since in the subj. opt., imper. inf., and part., as already shown, the aorist is always punctiliar and the so called present practically always linear, unless the Aktionsart of the verb itself is strongly punctiliar. (CF Discussion of the imper.) But in the indicative present the sharp line drawn between the imperf. and the aorist ind. (past time) does not exist. There is nothing left to do but divide the so called pres. ind. into Aoristic Present and Durative Present (or Punctiliar Present and Linear Present). The one Greek form covers both in the ind.... It is not wise therefore to define the pres. Ind. As denoting action in progress like the imperf.... Due to the failure in the development of separate tenses for punctiliar and linear action in the ind. of present time.[54]

Moulton says:

> ...the punctiliar force is obvious in certain presents.[55]

On page 879 under "indicative" Robertson says:

The Macmillan Co., 1923), 21-22.
53 H. P. V. Nunn, *A SHORT SYNTAX OF NEW TESTAMENT GREEK*, (Cambridge: University Press, 1912), 67.
54 Robertson, *A Grammar of the Greek New Testament*, 864.
55 James Hope Moulton, Nigel Turner, *A grammar of New Testament Greek*, 2nd edition, (London: SIMPKIN, MARSHALL, HAMILTON, KENT, and Co. LIMITED; New York: CHARLES SCRIBNER'S SONS; printed by Morrison & Gibb for T. & T. Clark, Edinburgh: T. & T. Clark, 1906), 119, accessed electronically via Google Play books, URL: https://books.google.com/books?id=Be4NAAAAIAAJ&pg=PR3&source=gbs_selected_pages&cad=2#v=onepage&q&f=false (accessed 6/29/17).

(a) The present for present time. It has already been seen that the durative sense does not monopolize the "present" tense; it more frequently denotes linear action. The verb and the context must decide.[56]

Dr. Carroll Osburn says:

> The attempt to require continuity in moichatai in verse 9 based upon the present tense is an abuse of Greek syntax resulting from a misunderstanding of Greek mood distinctions... -in the present indicative no clear distinction can be drawn from the tense between the action which is specifically ongoing and that which is not.[57]

Carroll Osburn says in *Restoration Quarterly*:

> Of the more than 700 instances of the present indicative in Matthew's Gospel, the vast majority of occurrences are "descriptive" with no continuity under consideration... [58]

Jack McKinney, professor of Biblical languages at Harding University in Searcy, Arkansas, said in a personal letter to writer Olan Hicks:

> As you have pointed out, and as the grammars you cite confirm, to force the meaning "continues to commit adultery," or "goes on living in adultery," on this verse is grammatically wrong. - The commission of adultery is concurrent in time with the marrying, prefaced only upon the man's already having been married before.[59]

---

56 Robertson, *A Grammar of the Greek New Testament*, 879.
57 Osburn, "Interpreting Greek Syntax," in *Biblical Interpretation*, 237.
58 Carroll Osburn, "The Present Indicative in Matthew 19:9," *Restoration Quarterly*, 24, no. 4 (1981). Sources have mentioned the page numbers for this article as being 193-203, but the exact page of the quote is unknown to the author since the article was accessed electronically. Accessed electronically via the Abilene Christian University *Restoration Quarterly* archives. URL: http://www.acu.edu/legacy/sponsored/restoration_quarterly/archives/1980s/vol_24_no_4_contents/osburn.html (accessed 2/21/17).
59 Jack McKinney, personal letter to Olan Hicks. Quoted in Hicks, *WHAT THE BIBLE SAYS ABOUT MARRIAGE, DIVORCE, & REMARRIAGE*, 130.

Turner says:

> In order to say I walk without reference to time, English can be unambiguous; not so Greek. It must use the indicative of the present... Thus in Greek one seldom knows apart from context whether the pres. indic. means I walk or I am walking. In other moods than indic., of course, the problem does not arise... One must always bear that in mind for exegesis.[60]

The following are samplings of passages with words that are present tense, indicative mood, and punctiliar, not durative.[61]

Matthew 13:44 **Again, the kingdom of heaven is like unto treasure hid in a field; the which when a man hath found, he hideth, and for joy thereof goeth and <u>selleth</u>** (present active indicative) **all that he hath, and <u>buyeth</u>** (present active indicative) **that field.** The words "selleth and "buyeth" in this passage are both present indicative and the Aktionsart of both are point action, not durative; the man does not continue selling all he has nor does he keep on buying the field. Luke 11:17 **But he, knowing their thoughts, said unto them, Every kingdom divided against itself is brought to desolation; and a house divided against a house <u>falleth</u>** (present active indicative). The word "falleth" in this passage is present indicative and the Aktionsart (type of action) is point action, not durative; the house does not keep on falling. Matthew 8:31 **So the devils besought him, saying, If thou <u>cast</u>** (present active indicative) **us out, suffer us to go away into the herd of swine.** The word "cast" in this passage is present indicative and the Aktionsart is point action, not durative. The devils did not request to be in a perpetual casting out, but to be cast out once so they could enter the swine. Matthew 3:11 **I indeed baptize** (present indicative) **you with water unto repentance: but he that cometh after me is mightier than I, whose shoes**

---

60 Nigel Turner, *A GRAMMAR OF NEW TESTAMENT GREEK*, Volume III, *SYNTAX*, (Edinburgh: T. & T. Clark, 1963), 60. Although the authorship of the series of books is attributed to James Hope Moulton, Volume III was written by Nigel Turner.
61 In the passages in the following section, underlining and/or information about the Greek is added for emphasis and/or information.

I am not worthy to bear: he shall baptize you with the Holy Ghost, and with fire:. This is merely a declarative statement (i.e. a simple statement of fact) and does not denote action in progress. Matthew 8:25 **And his disciples came to him, and awoke him, saying, Lord, save us: we perish** (present indicative). This obviously does not refer to a continual perishing. Matthew 20:30 **And, behold, two blind men sitting by the way side, when they heard that Jesus passed by** (present indicative)**, cried out, saying, Have mercy on us, O Lord, thou Son of David.** Jesus did not continually pass by. See also the present indicative verbs in Matthew 13:44; 26:40, 63; and 27:63. Regardless of what some "Greek expert" might say, the bible shows that the word "adultery," based on context, is a point action.

One passage stands out as a major problem for the traditional view that the adultery is committed with the second wife. Luke 16:18 **Whosoever putteth away his wife, and marrieth another, committeth adultery: and whosoever marrieth her that is put away from her husband committeth adultery.** In this passage, the words translated "putteth away" and "marrieth another" are present participles in the Greek. The rules governing present participles are as follows:

J Gresham Machen:

> The tense of the participle is relative to the time of the leading verb. The present participle, therefore, is used if the action denoted by the participle is represented as taking place at the same time as the action denoted by the leading verb.[62]

Dana & Mantey:

> (2) Simultaneous action relative to the main verb is ordinarily expressed by the present.[63]

Daniel B. Wallace:

---
62 Machen, *NEW TESTAMENT GREEK FOR BEGINNERS*, 105.
63 Dana & Mantey, *A MANUAL GRAMMAR OF THE GREEK NEW TESTAMENT*, 230.

The present participle is used for *contemporaneous* time.[64]

Thus, the use of the present participle in this passage for "putteth away" and "Marrieth another" means simply these acts are seen as occuring simultaneously with the action denoted in the leading verb, which is "committeth adultery." In other words, the two acts of putting away and marrying another are seen as occurring at the same time as the "commits adultery." An example of this is 1 John 3:15 **Whosoever hateth his brother is a murderer: and ye know that no murderer hath eternal life abiding in him.** The word "hateth" is a present participle and the "being a murderer" occurs simultaneously. For example, if I said "the baseball player took his bat, swung and hit the ball and knocked it out of the park." The swinging and hitting would be seen as occurring simultaneous to knocking the ball out of the park. We would not say he swung the bat on Monday, hit the ball on Wednesday, and knocked it out of the park on Friday. The adultery is committed in the two acts of putting away and marrying another, and is committed against the first wife, not in the subsequent marriage relationship.

This passage poses another problem for the traditional view. According to the traditional view, as soon as one marriage partner commits adultery, the innocent spouse is free to remarry. The problem in this passage is the man is seen as divorcing and marrying another, thereby committing adultery, and then his wife marries another who then commits adultery by marrying her. How can that be? If the husband divorces his wife and marries another, thus committing adultery, the Matthean exception clause should go into effect, and the innocent wife should be free to remarry without sin! Someone might say "she remarries before the husband remarries." That will not do; the Greek grammar does not allow for that, nor does the English translation if taken just as it is written. In fact, one does not have to know Greek to see what is plainly stated in

---

64 Daniel B. Wallace, GREEK GRAMMAR BEYOND THE BASICS, An Exegetical Syntax of the New Testament, (Grand Rapids, MI: Zondervan Publishing, 1997 [1996 copyright date]), 614, accessed electronically via Amazon.com, URL: https://www.amazon.com/Greek-Grammar-Beyond-Basics-Exegetical/dp/0310218950 (accessed 3/6/17).

the English text. It is plain to see (in the first clause) that Jesus is envisioning a man putting away his wife and marrying another, followed (in the second clause) by the woman who was put away in this situation subsequently getting married. Both clauses in this passage cannot be true if the traditional teaching is true.

In Matthew 19:9, the words "put away" and "marry another" are aorist participles, and the leading verb "committeth adultery" is present indicative. Can aorist participles be seen as contemporaneous in time with a present indicative leading verb? The answer is yes; although aorist participles are usually antecedent[65] in time to the leading verb (unless the leading verb is also aorist), they can be seen as simultaneous action with the leading verb even if the verb is present indicative.

A.T. Robertson:

> One has no ground for assuming that antecedent action is a necessary or an actual fact with the aorist participle. <u>The aorist participle of simultaneous action is in perfect accord with the genius and history of the Greek participle</u> (p. 1113). The relative time of the participle approximates the indicative mode and is able to suggest antecedent (aorist, present, perfect tenses), <u>simultaneous (aorist, present tenses)</u> (p. 1111). <u>The coincident use of aorist tense occurs also with …the present</u> as as αποκριθεισ λεγει (Mk. 8:29).[66]

Mark 8:29 **And he asked them, But who say ye that I am? Peter <u>answereth and saith unto him</u>, Thou art the Christ** Notice also John 21:19 **Now this he spake, signifying by what manner of death he should glorify God. And when he had <u>spoken this, he saith</u> unto him, Follow me.**[67] Here we have Jesus telling Peter what manner of death he would die,

---

65 This means they are usually seen as occurring before the leading verb in time.
66 Robertson, *A Grammar of the Greek New Testament*, 861. Underlining added for emphasis.
67 Underlining and information about the Greek was added for emphases and/or information in the previous two passages.

and telling Peter along with the other disciples to follow Him. These two acts are seen as occurring simultaneous. We have an aorist participle "spoken" (*eipon*) with a present indicative leading verb "saith" (*legei*) both seen as occurring contemporaneous in time.

Furthermore, Matthew 19:9 is a conditional clause sentence. There are stipulated conditions given (the protasis), which are putting away and marrying another, and when these conditions occur, then the result (the apodosis) becomes a reality, which is adultery.

One last argument made by those who hold the traditional view, who know and read Greek, concerns the presence of the particle *an*[68] in Matthew 19:9. The claim is because of the presence of the particle, *moichao* must be continuous action. The presence of the particle, according to the traditional view, sees the man who puts away a wife and marrying another, committing adultery each and every time he has sexual relations with the second wife. The explanation to the presence of the particle is simple. Because this is a conditional clause sentence, the presence of the particle simply means that each and every time the protasis occurs (i.e. every time a man, any man, putts away his wife and marries another) the apodosis (adultery) becomes a reality in each and every occurrence (cf. Acts 2:38, 39).

Conclusion:

Matthew 5:32 **32 but I say unto you, that every one that putteth away his wife, saving for the cause of fornication, maketh her an adulteress: and whosoever shall marry her when she is put away committeth adultery.** (ASV) Notice "shall marry" is translated from the Greek word *gamese*. This word is aorist tense in the Greek which means it is viewed as point action, that is, it is not being viewed as a continuing or repeated action. Therefore, it does not refer to the practice of the husband-wife relationship which follows the "marrying."

---

[68] The particle *an* (αν) refers to a repeated action dependant on some circumstance or condition. (see Walter Bauer, William F. Arndt, and F. Wilbur Gingrich, A GREEK ENGLISH LEXICON OF THE NEW TESTAMENT, 47).

Terms you often hear are statements such as "if one divorces unscripturally and marries another, he or she is living in adultery" or "living in an adulterous marriage." None of these terms are scriptural terms. As we studied last time, a divorce is simply a divorce, just as a death certificate is simply a death certificate. The divorce does not kill the marriage; it is given because the marriage is dead. The bible does not use the terms "unscriptural divorce" or "an adulterous marriage."

We have examined some passages in light of the Greek. I must say, although I am a student of Greek, I am not a Greek scholar, nor do I claim to be. I have relied on the scholarship of others, and although some insights can certainly be gained through studying the Greek grammar, it is not necessary to know the Greek grammar to know what the bible says on the subject of MDR. The standard English translations are all we need to know and see the truth on this issue. It is simply a matter of accepting the text as it is stated. For example, Mark 10:11 **Whosoever shall put away his wife, and marry another, committeth adultery against her.** In this text we just need to understand "put away" means "put away" and "marry another" means "marry another," and when these two are done, then adultery is committed, and the adultery is committed "against her," that is, the man's first wife.

CHAPTER IV: THE SERMON ON THE MOUNT

How are we to understand Jesus' words in the Sermon on the Mount? Many in the church suppose that the purpose of the sermon was to set aside the Old Testament (OT) morality and to institute a new and distinctive ethic. He was, as it were, laying a trump on top of Moses. The gospel is seen as an elevation of morality over the OT. Marcion, very early in church history, even went so far as to say there were two different Gods. There was the OT God: legalistic, angry, and vindictive. This God was only about behavior modification. Then there is the God of the New Testament (NT): a God of love and a God concerned with the man's heart, not just about actions.[69] The problem with this thinking is the same God is behind both testaments. Was it not the God of the OT that said to Samuel; **But the LORD said unto Samuel, Look not on his countenance, or on the height of his stature; because I have refused him: for the LORD seeth not as man seeth; for man looketh on the outward appearance, but the LORD looketh on the heart.** (1 Samuel 16:7 KJV) God also said; **Hear, O Israel: The LORD our God is one LORD: And thou shalt love the LORD thy God with all thine heart, and with all thy soul, and with all thy might.** (Deuteronomy 6:4-5 KJV). There are indications that some in the first century were making this very charge against Jesus; in particular, the Jewish leaders of Jesus' day were accusing Jesus of opposing the Law of Moses. The truth is Jesus was not doing this at all, but was properly interpreting the ethics of the OT. The contrast is not between the Old Testament and the New Testament, as some suppose, but rather Jesus was contrasting the shallow and perverted interpretations of the Law by the scribes, Pharisees, and Rabbis of His day with the proper meaning and import of the Law.

---

[69] David E. Smith, *The Canonical Function of Acts: A Comparative Analysis*, (Collegeville, MN: The Liturgical Press, 2002 (copyright date [originally published 1963]), 44. Accessed online via *Google Books*. URL: https://books.google.com/books?id=bk8gRelhVv0C&printsec=frontcover&source=gbs_ge_summary_r&cad=0#v=onepage&q&f=false (accessed 3/7/17).

Notice Jesus did not begin by saying "it is written," but rather, "you have heard it was said" etc. He was not referring to what was actually written in the Law, rather He was referring to what was being said about the Law. Because Jesus contradicted the interpretation of the law and the prophets by the Jewish leaders of His day, and because they were accepted as the official interpreters of the OT, it was necessary that Jesus, in no uncertain terms, stress His agreement with the OT. Jesus did just that in His introduction to His series of contrasts. Matthew 5:17 **Think not that I came to destroy the law or the prophets: I came not to destroy, but to fulfil.**

There are three words that are of vital importance in understanding Jesus', statement. First is the word *katalusai* translated "destroy" meaning "to do away with, abolish, annul, make invalid."[70] Second is *plerosai* translated "fulfill" meaning, according to Thayer:

> To fulfill; i.e. to cause God's will (as made known in the Law) to be obeyed as it should be, and God's promises (given through the prophets) to receive fulfillment; Mt v. 17.[71]

Jesus is saying He is not destroying the Law and the prophets, but giving the full meaning of them. In verses 17 and 18 we have the words "fulfill" and fulfilled" (Matthew 5:17-18) **Think not that I am come to destroy the law, or the prophets: I am not come to destroy, but to fulfil. For verily I say unto you, Till heaven and earth pass, one jot or one tittle shall in no wise pass from the law, till all be fulfilled.**[72] The words appear to be the same in the English KJV, however, the word "fulfill" in verse 17 is a different Greek word than the word "fulfilled" in verse 18. The word in verse 18 is *genetai*. The word in verse 17 is *plerosai* and means *"to bring to full*

---

70 From the Greek *kataluo*. Walter Bauer, William F. Arndt, and F. Wilbur Gingrich, *A GREEK ENGLISH LEXICON OF THE NEW TESTAMENT and OTHER EARLY CHRISTIAN LITERATURE*, (Chicago: The University of Chicago Press, 1957), 415.
71 From the Greek *pleroo*. Joseph H. Thayer, *THAYER'S GREEK-ENGLISH LEXICON OF THE NEW TESTAMENT: Coded to Strong's Numbering System*, (2009), 518.
72 Underlining added.

expression = show it forth in its true *mng*" [meaning].[73] The word *genetai* in verse 18 means, according to Thayer, "to become i.q. to come to pass, happen, of events... univ.: Mt v. 18..."[74] The word *genetai* in verse 18 is referring to Jesus fulfilling the law on the cross whereas the word *plerosai* is speaking to Jesus giving the proper understanding or full meaning of the law (cf. Col. 1:25-26).

A few matters need understanding to see the truth of what Jesus is saying in relation to the Law.

First: Jesus is not quoting the law verbatim e.g. Matthew 7:12 **Therefore all things whatsoever ye would that men should do to you, do ye even so to them: for this is the law and the prophets.** This verse is not found in the OT, however, Jesus says "for this is the law and the prophets."

Second: to properly interpret scripture one must consider all that is said in scripture that relates to the subject in any context.

Allen Isbell says:

> To understand properly any phrase or precept, one must compare it with collateral scriptures. This is commonly known as the "analogy of faith" method... The analogy of faith method also shows that other controversial phrases in the same paragraph are not without qualifications. The command to give away the coat and cloak and the injunction to give to him who begs and not to refuse him who would borrow must be interpreted in the light of other instructions. For example a Christian is to provide first for his family, for, "if any one does not provide for his relatives, especially for his family, he has disowned the faith and is worst than an unbeliever" (1Tim. 5:8). Clearly obedience to Matthew 5:42 must be tempered by the obligation involved in 1 Timothy 5:8. Moreover, the analogy of

---

[73] From the Greek *pleroo*. Walter Bauer, William F. Arndt, and F. Wilbur Gingrich, *A GREEK ENGLISH LEXICON OF THE NEW TESTAMENT*, 677.
[74] From the Greek *ginomai*. Joseph H. Thayer, *THAYER'S GREEK-ENGLISH LEXICON OF THE NEW TESTAMENT: Coded to Strong's Numbering System*, (2009), 115.

faith method shows that there are occasions when the Christian must refuse to give to those who ask. Christians are not to support those who prefer idleness to work "if any will not work, let them not eat," (2 Thess. 3:6-12)... Christians are not to give to those who do not abide in the doctrine of Christ (2 John 1:10, 11). What if a heretic demanded our church buildings, homes and money, are we to give these to him?... Jesus' words were for the spiritual welfare of the disciple and not for the encouragement of injustice of wickedness.[75]

Third: we must be careful to distinguish between moral principles as they pertain to civil authorities and to the individual. Some things done by a civil society are morally right, but when done by an individual they are not morally right. Israel was a theocracy; therefore many of the instructions given were in reference to the protection of a sovereign nation (defined by physical boundaries) as opposed to instructions in regards to the actions of an individual. Concerning the individual, God has never thought any different about how we are to treat our fellow man. The weightier matters of the law, both old and new, have always been judgment, mercy, and faith (Matthew 23:23). God's moral ethics are consistent through the ages.

By examining the "contrast statements" of Jesus in the Sermon on the Mount, we shall be able to draw some conclusions as to the nature of the contrasts. Is He really changing the moral ethics in the Old law to a new and elevated ethics system, or is He restoring the law to the ethical standard of God that had been corrupted and diluted by the religious leaders of Israel?

Matthew 5:21-22 Ye have heard that it was said to them of old time, Thou shalt not kill; and whosoever shall kill shall be in danger of the judgment: but I say unto you, that every one who is angry with his brother shall be in danger of the judgment; and whosoever shall say to his brother, Raca, shall be in danger of the council; and whosoever shall say, Thou fool, shall be in danger of the hell of fire.

---
75 Allen C. Isbell, *WAR AND CONSCIENCE*, (Abilene, TX: Biblical Research Press, 1966), 25-32.

The Jewish leaders had interpreted the commandment "thou shalt not kill" to be limited to the physical act of murder itself; anything short of the willful, unlawful taking of life was not considered to be in violation of the sixth commandment. Jesus makes a much broader application to include hateful and bitter feelings and words. Is this new teaching or was this taught in the Old Testament?

Leviticus 19:17-18 **Thou shalt not hate thy brother in thy heart: thou shalt surely rebuke thy neighbor, and not bear sin because of him. Thou shalt not take vengeance, nor bear any grudge against the children of thy people; but thou shalt love thy neighbor as thyself: I am Jehovah.** Certainly the Old Testament condemned hateful, bitter feelings and words.

Matthew 5:27-28 **Ye have heard that it was said, Thou shalt not commit adultery: but I say unto you, that every one that looketh on a woman to lust after her hath committed adultery with her already in his heart.** Once again, as with the sixth commandment, the Jewish leaders interpreted the commandment "thou shalt not commit adultery" to be limited to the physical act. Jesus says the breaking of the marriage covenant is not limited to the physical act, but is actually committed in the heart first. Again, is this new teaching or was this taught in the Old Testament? Exodus 20:17 **Thou shalt not covet thy neighbor's wife. Proverbs 6:24-27 To keep thee from the evil woman, From the flattery of the foreigner's tongue. Lust not after her beauty in thy heart; Neither let her take thee with her eyelids. For on account of a harlot a man is brought to a piece of bread; And the adulteress hunteth for the precious life. Can a man take fire in his bosom, And his clothes not be burned?** Once again we see Jesus was teaching that which is found in the Old Testament.

Matthew 5:38-39 **Ye have heard that it was said, An eye for an eye, and a tooth for a tooth: but I say unto you, resist not him that is evil: but whosoever smiteth thee on thy right cheek, turn to him the other also.**

Allen Isbell says:

> Is it asserted that Jesus abrogated the moral right of the state to punish criminals and to avenge injustice when he said "Ye have heard that it was said, an eye for an eye, and a tooth for a tooth: but I say unto you, resist not him that is evil?" The cause of misunderstanding is plain. The Old Testament did use the "eye for an eye" terminology (Exodus 21:23; Leviticus 24:17-21; Deuteronomy 19:21), however, each context shows that this was a judicial principle, given for the purpose of insuring that the punishment of the criminal would be commensurate with the crime. The "eye for an eye" statements were never intended to license the individual to carry out vendettas or to avenge his own injuries or to rectify injustice apart from the judicial apparatus of society. Rather, the individual was expressly prohibited from personally extracting an eye for an eye. The Old Testament says, "Do not say, I will do to him as he has done to me; I will pay the man back for what he has done," (Proverbs 24:29). To understand the Old Testament (and, hence, to understand what Jesus had in mind) this verse must be harmonized with Exodus 21:23. That a harmonization is possible may be seen by the following illustration: X steals sheep from Y. Exodus 21:23 did not license Y to avenge personally his loss by stealing sheep from X. As an individual, he was under the restraints of Proverbs 24:29. However, since X's action was a crime against society, as well as against Y personally the judicial system was established by which society could avenge this crime by impartially decreeing a punishment commensurate with the crime i.e. an eye for an eye. Hence, Proverbs 24:29 and Exodus 21:23 complement each other. The importance of one's understanding the intent of the Sermon on the Mount is now brought into clear focus. If Jesus is putting his teachings against the Old Testament system, then his rejection of "eye for eye" concept makes it necessary for us to conclude that society

no longer has a moral right to avenge injustice or to punish a public crime. But if Jesus is interpreting properly the Old Testament code, this conclusion does not follow. When Jesus used the "eye for an eye" terminology, he was rejecting the common belief that the individual had the right to avenge personally his enemies by extracting an eye for an eye... Jesus had this perverted teaching in mind and was denying the individual what was always denied him-the right to seek vengeance personally. However, it does not follow that Jesus denied the right of society to remedy social injustice and to resist the criminals and wrongdoers.[76]

Romans 13:3-4 **For rulers are not a terror to good works, but to the evil. Wilt thou then not be afraid of the power? do that which is good, and thou shalt have praise of the same: For he is the minister of God to thee for good. But if thou do that which is evil, be afraid; for he beareth not the sword in vain: for he is the minister of God, a revenger to execute wrath upon him that doeth evil.**

Proverbs 24:29 **Say not, I will do so to him as he hath done to me; I will render to the man according to his work.** We can see the Old Testament forbids an eye for an eye by the individual, and the New Testament approves of an eye for an eye by the civil government, and this is in harmony with the teachings of Jesus. Certainly the Kingdom of God today is not a physical nation with borders, etc., but the indication from scripture is that Christians may even participate as agents of the citizenry. They may be judges, soldiers, police officers etc. (Luke 3:14, Acts 10:1-2) The question to be asked is: has God changed His position on moral ethics from the Old Testament to the New? We must ask ourselves: is it merciful and loving to allow an innocent victim to be brutally beaten or killed? To whom are we being merciful and loving? Had the Good Samaritan come upon the robbers as they were beating the man from Jerusalem, what should he have done? Paul resisted those who intended to take his life by appealing to the civil author-

---
[76] Ibid., 31-32.

ities for protection (Acts 23:16-24). Paul knew full-well that if his aggressors continued in their plan to kill him the armed Roman soldiers would have used deadly force to protect him.

Matthew 5:43-44 Ye have heard that it was said, Thou shalt love thy neighbor, and hate thine enemy: but I say unto you, love your enemies, and pray for them that persecute you;

Allen Isbell says:

> It would seem that the statement to "hate your enemy" was a perverted interpretation of Leviticus 19:17 which the scribes and Pharisees were foisting upon the people. As Lenski writes "with their vicious corollary about hating our enemies, the scribes and Pharisees had... fallen from the ancient moral height." Jesus was leading the people back to the moral summit by focusing attention to the true understanding of the Old Testament's morality.[77]

What did the Old Testament have to say about one's enemy? (Exodus 23:4-5) **If thou meet thine enemy's ox or his ass going astray, thou shalt surely bring it back to him again. If thou see the ass of him that hateth thee lying under his burden, and wouldest forbear to help him, thou shalt surely help with him.** (Proverbs 25:21-22) **If thine enemy be hungry, give him bread to eat; and if he be thirsty, give him water to drink: For thou shalt heap coals of fire upon his head, and the LORD shall reward thee.** (Leviticus 19:17-18) **Thou shalt not hate thy brother in thine heart: thou shalt in any wise rebuke thy neighbour, and not suffer sin upon him. Thou shalt not avenge, nor bear any grudge against the children of thy people, but thou shalt love thy neighbour as thyself: I am the LORD.** A very important statement is made by Jesus in the Sermon on the Mount; in fact it is the crux of all that Jesus had to say. (Matthew 5:17-20) **Think not that I came to destroy the law or the prophets: I**

---
77 Ibid., 30. Isbell quoted R. C. H. Lenski, *THE INTERPRETATION OF ST. MATHEW'S GOSPEL*, (Columbus, OH: The Warburg Press, 1943), 246.

came not to destroy, but to fulfil. For verily I say unto you, Till heaven and earth pass away, one jot or one tittle shall in no wise pass away from the law, till all things be accomplished. Whosoever therefore shall break one of these least commandments, and shall teach men so, shall be called least in the kingdom of heaven: but whosoever shall do and teach them, he shall be called great in the kingdom of heaven. <u>For I say unto you, that except your righteousness shall exceed the righteousness of the scribes and Pharisees, ye shall in no wise enter into the kingdom of heaven.</u>**[78]** The righteousness of the Pharisees consisted of a perverted, shallow, and superficial interpretation of the Old Testament Law that focused primarily on behavioral modification. Jesus was calling for all to come to the knowledge of the truth of the teachings of the Old Testament. God has always had the goal of having people to worship from the heart and to have good moral character.

You may have noticed Matthew 5:31-32 has conspicuously been left out. That is because we shall deal with this passage in detail in chapter seven.

---

78 Underlining added for emphasis.

CHAPTER V: POLYGAMY AND JESUS' AUDIENCE

Matthew 19:4-5 And he answered and said unto them, Have ye not read, that he which made them at the beginning made them male and female, And said, For this cause shall a man leave father and mother, and shall cleave to his wife: and they twain shall be one flesh?

1 Timothy 4:1-3 Now the Spirit speaketh expressly, that in the latter times some shall depart from the faith, giving heed to seducing spirits, and doctrines of devils; Speaking lies in hypocrisy; having their conscience seared with a hot iron; Forbidding to marry.

WHAT ABOUT POLYGYNY:

There are four words in reference to the number of marriage partners one may have. It will be important in this section of study to recognize the difference in meanings between them. The following definitions are from the Collins English Dictionary.

Monogamy: the state or practice of having only one husband or wife over a period of time[79]

Polygamy: the practice of having more than one wife or husband at the same time[80]

Polygyny: the practice or condition of being married to more than one wife at the same time[81]

Polyandry: the practice or condition of being married to more

---

[79] *Collins English Dictionary - Complete & Unabridged 10th Edition*, s.v. "monogamy," HarperCollins Publishers, *Dictionary.com*. URL: http://www.dictionary.com/browse/monogamy (accessed: 3/8/17).
[80] Ibid., s.v. "polygamy," HarperCollins Publishers, *Dictionary.com*. URL: http://www.dictionary.com/browse/polygamy (accessed: 3/8/17).
[81] Ibid., s.v. "polygyny," HarperCollins Publishers, *Dictionary.com*. URL: http://www.dictionary.com/browse/polygyny (accessed: 3/8/17).

than one husband at the same time[82]

Polygamy, for those of us in 21st century America, is not a pressing issue since it is illegal and considered wrong by most. In fact, it is illegal in most countries in the world. However, in the two countries where we have the greatest missionary presence, Nigeria and India, polygyny is legal. Issues with polygyny in these countries should cause us to be interested in this subject, and perhaps there needs to be more open discussion about polygamy.

What I am going to attempt to present to you are simply the facts as they are presented in scripture in regards to polygamy. I will leave it to you to consider the facts and draw your own conclusions.

It is obvious God's ideal is a one-man, one-woman arrangement from the following facts. God introduced marriage as a monogamous relationship and He defined marriage in terms of monogamy.

Genesis 2:24 **Therefore shall a man** (singular) **leave his father and his mother, and shall cleave unto his wife** (singular)**: and they shall be one flesh.**

In scripture, every indication points to monogamy as God's preference for marriage. The fact that the first case of polygamy recorded is found among those who did not follow God should not go unnoticed. No case of polygamy is recorded among God's people down to the time of the flood. Of the eight persons saved in the ark, all eight were monogamous. In fact, it was not until many generations after Adam and Eve that the first recorded instance of polygyny is found among God's people. Interestingly enough, the first recorded case was with Abraham, the father of the faithful. When God speaks of marriage in the general sense, He speaks in monogamous terms. God also requires any man appointed to the office of Elder to be in a monogamous marriage; he is to be a one-woman man.

---
[82] Ibid., s.v. "polyandry," HarperCollins Publishers, URL: *Dictionary.com*. http://www.dictionary.com/browse/polyandry (accessed: 3/8/17).

Christ has only one bride.[83]

Having noticed these facts, we must also consider the fact that when polygyny began to be practiced among God's people it was not seen as a transgression of any known law of God. Polygyny just appears in scripture without any special attention given to its practice. There is no indication in scripture that polygyny is viewed as immoral or a corrupted way of life. There are no express statements in the bible, New or Old Testament, condemning polygyny. Polygyny is not seen as being approved or disapproved of in scripture. Solomon had 700 wives and 300 concubines and yet God never expressed any disapproval of him for having multiple wives. The only disapproval did not pertain to multiple marriages, but rather to other evils associated with them, such as the wives of Solomon turning his heart away from God. One other very important fact- polygyny is never referred to or even hinted at as being adultery. No passage of scripture equates polygyny to adultery. Notice adultery is condemned in Exodus 20:14: **Thou shalt not commit adultery.** However, God gives instruction concerning a man having more than one wife (i.e. polygyny) in Exodus 21:10: **If he take him another wife; her food, her raiment, and her duty of marriage, shall he not diminish.** as well as Deuteronomy 21:15-17: **If a man have two wives, one beloved, and another hated, and they have born him children, both the beloved and the hated; and if the firstborn son be hers that was hated: Then it shall be, when he maketh his sons to inherit that which he hath, that he may not make the son of the beloved firstborn before the son of the hated, which is indeed the firstborn: But he shall acknowledge the son of the hated for the firstborn, by giving him a double portion of all that he hath: for he is the beginning of his strength; the right of the firstborn is his.**

There are two passages some say are references to polygamy: 1 Corinthians 7:2 and Romans 7:1-3. Let us examine these two passages and see if we can determine in what way, if any, they relate to polygamy.

---
83 Revelation 21:9

1 Corinthians 7:2 **Nevertheless, to avoid fornication, let every man have his own wife, and let every woman have her own husband.**

This passage is said to speak to polygamy by way of inference because of the fact this verse says "man" singular and "woman" singular. However, the same inference could be drawn from Genesis 2:24 **Therefore shall a man leave his father and his mother, and shall cleave unto his wife: and they shall be one flesh.** Both man and wife are singular. As a matter of fact, when Jesus quoted this verse in Matthew 9:5, He added the word "two" indicating that is what God meant, one man one woman. But, as we know, faithful men of God practiced polygyny without a hint of disfavor from God. This truth goes without question to most serious bible students.

The Corinthian passage is not said in the context of what constitutes a lawful or unlawful marriage. If Paul had said "every marriage is to be one man with one woman," polygamy would certainly be inferred as unlawful by the context. The context of Paul's statement is avoiding fornication. Marriage is given as the solution to fornication. This passage is considered by many as a new covenant passage rather than a gnomic truth (i.e. a statement of fact or a timeless truth). The truth stated is: if someone who cannot contain wants to avoid fornication, he should get married. Is this limited to the NT saints, meaning it is only true for us in the NT age? Was it not also true for the OT saints? Were the OT saints different from us today pertaining to sexual appetites? 1 Corinthians 7:9 **but if they cannot exercise self-control, let them marry. For it is better to marry than to burn with passion.** (NKJV) Did people not also burn with passion before the cross? The solution to avoid fornication was the same for the OT saints as it is for the NT saints. Yet polygyny was certainly not forbidden to the OT saints under The Law. Marriage has always been the solution to avoiding fornication. When God created man, He made a woman for him because the animals were not suitable. Neither was another man suitable, nor did He create two women. No, He created one woman and the institution of marriage. Marriage has been, and is now, and (as long as this earth stands) will always be the solution to avoiding fornication. This principle is not just for those in the church, but for all people. Some say people in the world cannot sin against marriage because God does not regulate marriages of those in the world, rather all His words concerning marriage apply only to people in the covenant. But is this true? Those outside of Christ can and do commit both fornication and adultery. Notice 1 Corinthians 6:9-11: **Know ye not that the unrighteous shall not inherit the kingdom of God? Be not deceived: neither <u>fornicators</u>, nor idolaters, nor <u>adulterers</u>, nor effeminate, nor abusers of themselves with mankind, 10 Nor thieves, nor covetous, nor drunkards, nor revilers, nor extortioners, shall inherit the kingdom of God. 11 <u>And such were some of you</u>: but ye are washed, but ye are sanctified, but ye are justified in the name of the Lord Jesus, and by the Spirit of our God.**[84] Some of the Corinthians committed fornication before becoming Christians, but not all of them. Why not all of them? Because some were faithfully married or celibate.

Why did not Paul say "let every man have his own wives and every woman her own husbands"? A possible reason for saying "wife" (singular) and "husband" (singular) is because that is all that is necessary to avoid fornication. God created Eve for Adam and turned a "not good" situation into a "very good" situation. Eve was sufficient to meet the needs of Adam. For example, to kill a deer it takes one shot to the lungs. One bullet to the lungs is all that is necessary. You could shoot the deer three times in the lungs, but that would not be the proper way to tell someone what is needed to kill a deer since the deer would be dead after the first shot.

What about the word "own" as in "own wife" and "own husband"? The words translated "own" are not the same words in Greek in respect to the husband and to the wife. The word "own" in respect to the wife is the Greek word *idios*, and is a

---

84 Underlining added for emphasis.

possessive pronoun and means "one's own." The word "own" as it pertains to the man is the Greek word *heautou*. This word is a reflexive pronoun and means "to do something to or for oneself" or refers to that which pertains to oneself. This word is often translated "himself" (c.f. Luke 15: 17; 18: 11). This passage could be properly translated 1 Corinthians 7:2 **Nevertheless, to avoid fornication, let every man have *himself* a wife, and let every woman have her own husband.**

Now, let us examine Romans 7:1-4 **Know ye not, brethren, (for I speak to them that know the law,) how that the law hath dominion over a man as long as he liveth? For the woman which hath an husband is bound by the law to her husband so long as he liveth; but if the husband be dead, she is loosed from the law of her husband. So then if, while her husband liveth, she be married to another man, she shall be called an adulteress: but if her husband be dead, she is free from that law; so that she is no adulteress, though she be married to another man. Wherefore, my brethren, ye also are become dead to the law by the body of Christ; that ye should be married to another, even to him who is raised from the dead, that we should bring forth fruit unto God.**

What many fail to see in these verses is the fact that this passage is describing the condition of a woman[85] under the law **(for I speak to them that know the law... for the woman).**[86] However, many apply this passage to both men and women, that is, people in general. For a woman to have more than one husband is called polyandry in terms of the opposite, polygyny (a man having more than one wife) is never seen as adultery. Polyandry, a woman having more than one husband at a time, however, is adultery. There are no recorded examples of polyandry (that I am aware of) in the word of God among God's people. Why would polyandry be considered adultery while polygyny is not? The answer given in Romans 7

---

85 The Greek word for "wife," gune, occurs about 200 times in the New Testament and not once is it used in a generic sense (i.e. referring to both men and women). It always refers specifically to mature females.
86 The context shows this to be referring to The Law of Moses, see verses four and five.

is: **For the woman which hath an husband** (*hupandros*) **is bound by the law to her husband so long as he liveth.** The woman is to be in subjection to her husband and under his authority. (*hupandros* - This word occurs here only in the N.T. and means in subjection under a man, i.e. a married woman, Strongs #5220)[87]

Ephesians 5:22-24 **Wives, submit yourselves unto your own husbands, as unto the Lord. For the husband is the head of the wife, even as Christ is the head of the church: and he is the saviour of the body. Therefore as the church is subject unto Christ, so let the wives be to their own husbands in every thing.** A wife cannot be in subjection, or faithful, to two husbands at the same time- that would be confusion. The point made in Romans 7:1-4 is a nation of people cannot be subject or faithful to two laws at the same time just as a wife cannot be in subjection or faithful to two husbands at the same time.

Notice: Jeremiah 3:8 **And I saw, when for all the causes whereby backsliding Israel committed adultery I had put her away, and given her a bill of divorce; yet her treacherous sister Judah feared not, but went and played the harlot also.**

Here, we see God previously married to both Israel and Judah (see also Ezekiel 23:1-4), which was acceptable, but Israel was not allowed to have more than one "husband," or God, or else she would commit adultery. Exodus 20:3 **Thou shalt have no other gods before me.** The reason for polyandry being adultery is set forth by the principle found in Luke 16:13a: **No servant can serve two masters...** A woman (in this case Israel or Judah) could not be faithful to two masters at the same time (i.e. the Law of Moses and the law of Christ). In like manner, a wife cannot be faithful to or serve two masters at the same time.

Polygyny is not adultery whereas polyandry is adultery, but

---

87 James Strong, STRONG'S EXHAUSTIVE CONCORDANCE OF THE BIBLE,

(Nashville, TN: ThomasNelson Publishers, 1979), 505

even though polygyny is not adultery it is plain by the general tenor of the bible that God's ideal is one man with one woman for life.

God's regulations concerning polygyny seem to be concerned with justice and fair treatment rather than the number of wives. Notice Exodus 21:10 **If he take him another wife; her food, her raiment, and her duty of marriage, shall he not diminish.**[88]

God certainly spoke with favor in regards to monogamy, but with polygyny He did not speak in terms of favor or disfavor. Certainly one woman with one man is presented in scripture as the ideal arrangement for the needs of both the man and the woman to be met. God created one woman for Adam, not two or more, and said it was very good.

During Jesus' ministry Jesus was silent on the subject of polygyny. The apostles were also silent; they never mention polygyny. For sure at the time of Jesus a man could have more than one wife since Jesus lived under the law. This presents a major problem for the traditional view. Whether a man was still bound to a divorced wife and married to another would be irrelevant since the man could be bound to two wives without God's disapproval. Polygyny was certainly not adultery or unlawful, for he could be lawfully married to both women. This fact would not have been denied by anyone present during Jesus' discourse with the Pharisees on the subject of putting away one's wife.

WAS JESUS TEACHING NEW TESTAMENT MATTERS?

There are three possible explanations to the statements of Jesus.

> 1. Jesus' statements were strictly concerning the Old Testament. We should not take the statements of Jesus in the Gospel accounts and try to make application of them in the New Testament.

---
[88] See also Deuteronomy 21:15-17.

2. Jesus' statements were strictly concerning the New Testament. Jesus' teachings were contrary to the Old Law because He was teaching God's law as it would be enforced under the New Covenant that was to come in the future.

3. Jesus' statements are statements of facts- facts about God's moral code as it relates to the one flesh relationship and marriage. Jesus is revealing to us, as He did to all who have gone before and to all those who will follow, what God thinks about the marriage covenant and the breaking of the same. His statements would apply in the Old and New covenant.

Concerning number one: Since Paul said **And unto the married I command, yet not I, but the Lord...** (1 Corinthians 7:10a), obviously some of what Jesus said was applicable in the New Testament. However, because the Law of Moses is specifically mentioned in this context, it cannot be true that Jesus' statements are exclusively concerning the New Testament.

Concerning number two: Since the Law of Moses was specifically mentioned in this context, it is self-evident that the Law of Moses is being discussed. However, because the apostle Paul applied Jesus' teaching to Christians, the statements of Jesus cannot be exclusively concerning the Old Testament.

Concerning number three: Since the statements of Jesus apply to the Old and New Testament, then number three must be the logical explanation.

The question we want to examine is whether or not Jesus' statements were strictly NT teaching and meant to be instructions to a future people in a future dispensation. This is the predominant position taken by those who hold the traditional view in the church.

One of the ways to come to a proper understanding of God's word is through certain principles or rules of bible interpretation called hermeneutics. It is interesting to me that some of the most learned men in proper bible hermeneutics ignore these basic rules when it comes to the subject of MDR. Three of the most fundamental rules to proper interpretation of the bible are:

First: who is speaking?

Second: to whom is the speaker speaking?

Third: About what is the speaker speaking?

Let us examine the text based on these rules of bible interpretation and see what conclusions can be drawn.

Matthew 19:3-9 **The Pharisees also came unto him, tempting him, and saying unto him, Is it lawful for a man to put away his wife for every cause? And he answered and said unto them, Have ye not read, that he which made them at the beginning made them male and female, And said, For this cause shall a man leave father and mother, and shall cleave to his wife: and they twain shall be one flesh? Wherefore they are no more twain, but one flesh. What therefore God hath joined together, let not man put asunder. They say unto him, Why did Moses then command to give a writing of divorcement, and to put her away? He saith unto them, Moses because of the hardness of your hearts suffered you to put away your wives: but from the beginning it was not so. And I say unto you, Whosoever shall put away his wife, except it be for fornication, and shall marry another, committeth adultery: and whoso marrieth her which is put away doth commit adultery.**

Who is speaking? Jesus. To whom is Jesus speaking? The Pharisees. About what are they speaking? The Law of Moses. What are we asked to believe from those who hold the traditional view? We are being told Jesus was asked a question by some Pharisees about Moses' Law as it pertains to marriage and Jesus ignored the question (and those who asked the question), and gave instructions to another group of people about a law not yet in force. We are also asked to accept the fact that the Pharisees heard this new teaching and were silent, offering no protest. This would be quite remarkable, if true, considering the fact that the Pharisees did not accept Jesus as having the authority to set aside the law and introduce His own: John 10:33 **The Jews answered him, saying, For a good work we stone thee not; but for blasphemy; and because that thou, being a man, makest thyself God.** Note their purpose for asking the question in the first place was to tempt Jesus (i.e. catch Him contradicting the law). There can be no doubt from the context that Jesus' teaching was concerning the law of Moses, directed to the Jews, and was therefore applicable to them.

Consider what Jesus would have just said to these Pharisees if the traditional view is correct. Put yourself in the Pharisees' shoes as we examine what Jesus said to them.

First: Jesus is saying (according to the traditional view) if a man divorces his wife and marries another he commits adultery. The reason being, God does not recognize the divorce of the first wife as valid- He sees them as still married- therefore, God does not recognize the marriage of the second wife as valid because the man already has a wife. What Jesus would have done (assuming this were true) is renounce polygyny and declare it unlawful, which these Jews would have seen as lawful (and rightfully so because it was). Jesus would have just condemned some of the greatest heroes of the Jewish people as adulterers: people such as Abraham, Jacob, David, and Solomon. Jesus would have just condemned a good number of the population of the Jews then living as adulterers. Yet what do we hear from these Pharisees? Nothing; not a word is recorded as being spoken against nor recorded elsewhere in the Bible about this seemingly bold condemnation of the practice of polygyny. Later, even at His trial when accusers were being sought to accuse Him, not one came forward to make this charge against Jesus.

Second: Jesus is saying (according to the traditional view) that divorce is a sin. This would be in direct contradiction to the Law of Moses. Deuteronomy 24:1 says: **When a man taketh a wife, and marrieth her, then it shall be, if she find no favor in his eyes, because he hath found some unseemly thing in her, that <u>he shall write her a bill of divorcement, and give it in her hand</u>, and send her out of his house.** (ASV)[89] Jesus said this was a commandment from God. Mark 10:3-5 says: **And he answered and said unto them, What did <u>Moses command you</u>? And they said, Moses suffered to write a bill of divorcement, and to put her away. And Jesus answered and said unto them, For the hardness of your heart he wrote you this precept.**[90] Yet what do we hear from these Pharisees? Nothing. Not a word of protest is recorded in scripture. Not at this time nor later, not even at His trial when accusers were being sought to accuse Him did one come forward and make this charge against Jesus. This would be exactly what these Pharisees were looking for, that is, Jesus contradicting the law. It is reasonable to think they would have seized the moment to accuse Jesus of teaching things contrary to the law.

Third: Jesus is saying (according to the traditional view) if a man divorces his wife and she marries another then adultery is committed. This would be a direct contradiction of the law of Moses Deuteronomy 24:1-2 **When a man hath taken a wife, and married her, and it come to pass that she find no favour in his eyes, because he hath found some uncleanness in her: then let him write her a bill of divorcement, and give it in her hand, and send her out of his house. And when she is departed out of his house, <u>she may go and be another man's wife</u>.**[91] Jesus would have declared a part of the law sinful (i.e. a command of God to be adultery) but Paul said in Romans 7:7, **What shall we say then? Is the law sin?**

---

89 Underlining added for emphasis.
90 Ibid.
91 Ibid.

God forbid. Nay, I had not known sin, but by the law: for I had not known lust, except the law had said, Thou shalt not covet. Yet what do we hear from these Pharisees? Nothing. Not a word of protest is recorded in scripture. Not at this time nor later, not even at His trial when accusers were being sought to accuse Him did one come forward and make this charge against Jesus. This would be exactly what these Pharisees were looking for, that is, Jesus contradicting the law. It is reasonable to think they would have seized the moment to accuse Jesus of teaching things contrary to the law and expose Him as an imposter.

Fourth: Jesus is saying (according to the traditional view) if a man divorces his wife and marries another and his former wife marries another then to make it right the man must divorce his second wife and his former wife must divorce her second husband and they must remarry one another. This would also be in direct contradiction to the law of Moses Deuteronomy 24:3-4 **And if the latter husband hate her, and write her a bill of divorcement, and giveth it in her hand, and sendeth her out of his house; or if the latter husband die, which took her to be his wife; Her former husband, which sent her away, may not take her again to be his wife, after that she is defiled; for that is abomination before the LORD: and thou shalt not cause the land to sin, which the LORD thy God giveth thee for an inheritance.**[92] Jesus says that which God calls an "abomination" is now recommended to be done! Yet what do we hear from these Pharisees? Nothing. Not a word of protest is recorded in scripture. Not at this time nor later, not even at His trial when accusers were being sought to accuse Him did one come forward and make this charge against Jesus. So, that which God allowed (polygyny) is declared to be sin by Jesus, and that which God commanded (a writing of divorcement to be given) is declared to be sin by Jesus, and that which is said a woman may lawfully do (go be another man's wife) is proclaimed by Jesus, to be sin, and that which is said to be sin (a man marrying a former wife who has

---
92 Ibid.

been married to another i.e an abomination) is commanded to be done by Jesus; and yet there is no trace of evidence the Pharisees said anything in protest. The Pharisees sought diligently to find Him guilty of something for which they could accuse Him, yet there is no record the Jewish leaders charged Jesus with contradicting the law in this case.

Notice: Galatians 5:11 **And I, brethren, if I yet preach circumcision, why do I yet suffer persecution? then is the offence of the cross ceased.** If Jesus was teaching the traditional view contrary to the Law of Moses, then why was He not persecuted for it?!! When the Jews thought Jesus was teaching contrary to the Law of Moses in regards to the Sabbath day they persecuted him for it (John 5:16), but we find no such persecution for teaching against the marriage laws in Deuteronomy 24.[93]

JESUS WAS SPEAKING TO THE PHARISEES:

Matthew 19:5-6 **And said, For this cause shall a man leave father and mother, and shall cleave to his wife: and they twain shall be one flesh? Wherefore they are no more twain, but one flesh. What therefore God hath joined together, <u>let not man put asunder</u>.**[94] The Greek grammar indicates that this was something being done at the time and was ordered to be stopped. This verse uses a present imperative with the negative particle *me*.

A. T. Robertson says:

> In general *me* is used with the present imperative to forbid what one is already doing.[95]

Dana and Mantey says:

---
[93] This author realizes that we as students of God's word must be careful in drawing conclusions based on what is not said in scripture. It is possible the Pharisees could have protested but their objections were not recorded. One should not be dogmatic concerning those things that are not said. However this author believes the silence is significant. This author believes the questions raised are worthy of consideration and along with other evidence presented in this book, shows Jesus was not changing the law in regards to marriage (for example Matthew 5:18-19). The question regarding silence needed to be presented to the reader for consideration.
[94] Ibid.
[95] Robertson, *A Grammar of the Greek New Testament*, 890.

> The purpose of a prohibition, when expressed by the aorist subjunctive, is to forbid a thing before it has begun... But a prohibition in the present imperative means to forbid the continuance of an act; it commands to quit doing a thing.[96]

From this we can see Jesus was speaking to the Pharisees and we should apply His words to them. Jesus was referring to a practice being done contemporaneous in time to His teaching. To say Jesus was not speaking to these Pharisees is to ignore the Greek grammar. Another thing this tells us is it is possible to "put asunder" a marriage relationship. In other words, Jesus was not saying man cannot put asunder, but to the contrary He said some were doing just that and He was ordering it stopped. It would be unreasonable to think Jesus would be ordering something to be stopped that was not being done!

WHAT ABOUT LUKE 16:16?

Luke 16:16 **The law and the prophets were until John: since that time the kingdom of God is preached, and every man presseth into it.**

What does the phrase "the prophets were until John" mean in reference to time? Jesus always kept the Law and He never instructed His disciples to disobey the Law in any way, but always told them to observe the Law. Matthew 5:19 **Whosoever therefore shall break one of these least commandments, and shall teach men so, he shall be called the least in the kingdom of heaven: but whosoever shall do and teach them, the same shall be called great in the kingdom of heaven.** Jesus at no time claimed any portion of the Law to be sinful! Much of Jesus' teaching, in particular to those Jews, who opposed Him, was specifically about the law. For example, consider Jesus' instructions about the meaning of keeping the Sabbath Day (see Matthew 12:1ff, Mark 3:2ff, Luke 13:14ff, and John 5:9ff). Jesus gave instruction concerning the Law as it pertains to a man's obligation to his brother's widow (see Matthew 22:23-33). Sometimes, Jesus gave instruction that was just true

---
96 Dana & Mantey, *A MANUAL GRAMMAR OF THE GREEK NEW TESTAMENT*, 301.

and has been and is always true. For example, Matthew 22:21-22 says **They say unto him, Caesar's. Then saith he unto them, Render therefore unto Caesar the things which are Caesar's; and unto God the things that are God's. When they had heard these words, they marvelled, and left him, and went their way.** Of course Jesus' teaching to His disciples was often New Testament teaching i.e. about the kingdom to come (John 14:26). Even some of His teaching to those Jews who opposed Him was about the coming Kingdom (which He taught primarily in parables).

So what about: Luke 16:16 **The law and the prophets were until John: since that time the kingdom of God is preached, and every man presseth into it.**

Notice the context of this passage and especially the very next verse: Luke 16:17 **And it is easier for heaven and earth to pass, than one tittle of the law to fail.** Here is the very next verse: Luke 16:18 **Whosoever putteth away his wife, and marrieth another, committeth adultery: and whosoever marrieth her that is put away from her husband committeth adultery.** Reading these verses in context without the verse breaks, the passage reads this way: Luke 16:16-18 **The law and the prophets were until John: since that time the kingdom of God is preached, and every man presseth into it. And it is easier for heaven and earth to pass, than one tittle of the law to fail. Whosoever putteth away his wife, and marrieth another, committeth adultery: and whosoever marrieth her that is put away from her husband committeth adultery.**

What is the message Jesus is trying to send? The moral principles, those timeless principles that are right because they are right no matter what dispensation of time we are talking about, which have been revealed in the old Law, because they are timeless principles, would merge into the NT and become part of it. The broader context in which verses 16-18 are found is covetousness. These verses, I believe, relate to covetousness, and we shall explore that connection in chapter seven. Covetousness has always been wrong and is not right; it is not now, nor will it ever be. John's teaching was New Testament in so much as he was preparing people for the coming kingdom; however, he was not replacing the law. His words did not conflict in any way with those at that time keeping the law nor was he setting the law aside. John's teaching in no way was in conflict with the foundational principles of the law, especially those moral principles such as "thou shalt not covet." The point Jesus was making is, while John was teaching about the coming kingdom, at the same time the law was accomplishing its purpose. One of its purposes was to teach us what sin is. The particular sin in this context is covetousness. Notice what Paul says in Romans 7:7: **What shall we say then? Is the law sin? God forbid. Nay, I had not known sin, but by the law: for I had not known lust, except the law had said, Thou shalt not covet.** Jesus was correcting the abuse of Deuteronomy 24:1-4 as it pertained to covetousness, and as it was being practiced in Jesus' day.[97] The Pharisees of Jesus' day had perverted Deuteronomy 24 in order to justify their evil practice so that they might appear righteous before men. Luke 16:14-15 **And the Pharisees also, who were covetous, heard all these things: and they derided him. And he said unto them, Ye are they which justify yourselves before men; but God knoweth your hearts: for that which is highly esteemed among men is abomination in the sight of God.** John's teaching was to prepare people for the coming Kingdom. He was making them ready by telling them to repent. Matthew 3:1-2 **In those days came John the Baptist, preaching in the wilderness of Judaea, And saying, Repent ye: for the kingdom of heaven is at hand.** Jesus was telling these Pharisees; to be a part of the coming Kingdom, they needed to repent of their covetousness. The law would not fail as it pertained to moral principles and the defining of sin. One would have to embrace the moral principles revealed in the law, in order to be prepared to be a part of the Kingdom that was to come.

---

97 The connection between Jesus' comments about marriage and covetousness will be discussed in chapter seven.

CHAPTER VI: MATTHEW 19 AND "PUTTING AWAY" VERSUS "DIVORCE"

Matthew 19:5-6 And said, For this cause shall a man leave father and mother, and shall cleave to his wife: and they twain shall be one flesh? Wherefore they are no more twain, but one flesh. What therefore God hath joined together, <u>let not man put asunder</u>.[98]

1 Timothy 4:1-3 Now the Spirit speaketh expressly, that in the latter times some shall depart from the faith, giving heed to seducing spirits, and <u>doctrines of devils</u>; Speaking lies in hypocrisy; having their conscience seared with a hot iron; <u>Forbidding to marry</u>.[99]

God is for marriage-making and against marriage-breaking.

Robert Shank says:

> It is an unfortunate fact that many today, some of whom are completely sincere, are seriously hindered in their study of scripture through their failure to suppress preconceptions. At best, such can be done only imperfectly; and <u>it is true for all of us that, subjectively, the meaning of what we read and hear is conditioned to some extent by our preconceptions,</u> from which it is impossible to be wholly free. It is therefore helpful in our study of any passage of scripture to consult the original text and as many good translations as possible.[100]

Preconceptions are, in my estimation, the major problem in properly understanding Jesus' marriage statements. To illustrate my point I want to compare the traditional view with what is actually said by Jesus. It is apparent to me that the

---

98 Underlining added for emphasis.
99 Ibid.
100 Robert Shank, *LIFE IN THE SON: A Study of the Doctrine of Perseverance*, (Springfield, MO: Westcott Publishers, Springfield, Missouri, Ninth Printing, 1971 [original publication date 1960]), 121. Underlining added for emphasis.

traditional view denies every statement made by Jesus in the primary proof text usually used to support this view.

THE TRADITINAL VIEW DENIES THE WORDS OF JESUS!

JESUS SAYS: (Matthew 19:9a) **And I say unto you, Whosoever shall put away his wife, except for fornication...**

MAN SAYS: A man cannot put away his wife unless it is for fornication.

Jesus hypothesizes a situation where a man puts away his wife for a cause other than fornication. Man says, "that's impossible, a man cannot put away a wife unless it is for fornication." Jesus says any man ("whosoever") can put away a wife for a cause other than fornication and man says "no, man cannot put away his wife for a cause other than fornication." Man says exactly the opposite of what Jesus says!

JESUS SAYS: in Matthew 19:9b: **...and shall marry another...**

MAN SAYS: He cannot marry another.

Jesus says a man that puts away his wife for a cause other than fornication can marry another. Man says, "A man who puts away a wife for a cause other than fornication cannot marry another." Man says exactly the opposite of what Jesus says!

JESUS SAYS: in Matthew 19:9c: **...committeth adultery:...**

MAN SAYS: Adultery is not committed in putting away and marrying another but rather it is committed in later sex acts.

Jesus says: a man who puts away a wife for a cause other than fornication and marries another, commits adultery, but man says "he does not commit adultery by putting away one wife and marrying another, rather he commits adultery in subsequent sex acts later." Man denies Jesus' statement and adds something not stated by Jesus!

JESUS SAYS: in Matthew 19:9d: **...and whoso marrieth her which is put away...**

MAN SAYS: No man can marry a "put away" woman because she is not put away.

Jesus says that a man can marry a woman who is put away for a cause other than fornication. Man says a man cannot marry a woman put away for a cause other than fornication because she is not put away and it is impossible for another man to marry her. Man says exactly the opposite of what Jesus says!

JESUS SAYS: in Matthew 19:9e: **...doth commit adultery.**

MAN SAYS: The adultery is not committed in the marrying, but in the sex activity that follows.

Jesus says a man who marries a "put away" woman for a cause other than fornication commits adultery in marrying her. Man says he does not commit adultery by marrying a "put away" woman, rather he commits adultery in subsequent sex acts later. Man denies Jesus' statement and adds something not stated by Jesus!

Those who hold the traditional view do not accept the statements of Jesus just as they are stated. How is it that brothers and sisters in the church, men and women who are intelligent, logical thinking, God fearing people understand Jesus to say exactly the opposite of what He actually says? It is not because they do not love the truth; I believe they are honest truth-seekers. So why do they see these passages the way they do? It is because <u>we have been told</u> that when Jesus said "Whosoever shall put away his wife, except it be for fornication, and shall marry another" means that <u>he puts away his wife and marries another in the eyes of man, not in the eyes of God</u>. The vital question to be asked is *Who is saying this to us?* It does not say this in Matthew 19:3-9, Matthew 5:31-32, Mark 10:2-12, Luke 16:18, Romans 7:1-4, or in 1 Corinthians chapter 7. In fact, this is not said anywhere in scripture. If it does not come from scripture, it must come from man. It came from the Catholic Church and was set forth at the Council of Trent,[101] and men have been saying it ever since. I am not claiming my brothers and sisters accept the Catholic Church as authority, I am saying the Catholic Church is the source of this teaching. How can one understand Jesus to be saying something opposite of what He actually says? Simple- he or she comes to the statement of Jesus with traditional baggage i.e. a preconception. He or she has been conditioned to see the passage through the lens of traditional teaching. This preconception was the biggest obstacle to my seeing the marriage passages as a prohibition against marriage-breaking rather than a prohibition against marriage-making. It took a lot of personal thought and pondering before I was able to see the words of Jesus just as they are plainly stated. This paradigm shift has led me to believe Jesus said what He meant and He meant what He said. If someone says "what Jesus was saying was meant to be understood in how man sees it, not how God sees it," is it not our responsibility to ask for proof? Should we not request to be shown in scripture? Would it not be the responsible thing to do to kindly ask for evidence rather than accepting something that is merely told to us? 1 Thessalonians 5:21 says, **Prove all things; hold fast that which is good.** What would you think if a prominent Calvinist preacher were to say to you when Paul said in Galatians 5:4b, **...whosoever of you are justified by the law; ye are fallen from grace.**, he was talking about only in the eyes of man, not in the eyes of God? What if he told you "It is impossible for man to fall from grace in God's eyes, Paul was talking about a man losing his influence with man or was never a Christian in the eyes of God in the first place."? Would you accept that without scriptural validation? When Jesus says in Mark 10:11b **Whosoever shall put away his wife, and marry another, committeth adultery against**

---

101 See appendix B.

her: (ASV), should we accept the claim Jesus meant only in the eyes of man without scriptural confirmation? The reality is, every statement of God in scripture could be denied with this approach. We are not under any obligation to just accept a teaching because it is popular or because it is recognized to be true by some prominent preachers or certain recognized scholars. Man says, "a man cannot fall from grace; God saves him, only God can unsave him." Man also says, "a man cannot put away his wife; God marries them, only God can unmarry them." But what does the bible say? Jesus said, **Whosoever shall put away his wife...** Sounds like any man can put away his wife! (i.e. it is possible, not that God approves). The restoration principle "speak where the bible speaks and be silent where the bible is silent" is still a good rule of thumb.

Let us turn now and begin an examination of what Jesus says about MDR. We shall break down the statements of Jesus line by line, even word by word, if necessary. To understand what Jesus really said we will need to come to a proper understanding of four words in scripture.

1. The Hebrew word *shalach*- often translated "put away" in the Old Testament. Strong's defines this word as: "to send away... cast (away, out)...forsake...leave...push away, put (away, forth, in, out)...send (away, forth, out)."[102]

2. The Hebrew word *keriythuwth*- translated "divorcement" in the OT. Strong's defines this word as: "a cutting (of the matrimonial bond), i.e. divorce:--divorce(-ment)."[103]

3. The Greek word *apoluo*- translated "put away" in the New Testament. Bauer, Arndt, and Gingrich give as the primary meaning of this word: "set free, release, pardon," secondarily "let go, send away, dismiss." Under the second mean-

---
102 James Strong, *STRONG'S EXHAUSTIVE CONCORDANCE OF THE BIBLE*, (Nashville, TN: Thomas Nelson Publishers, 1979), 116.
103 Ibid., 57.

ing they add the use of the word as "divorce."[104]

4. The Greek word *apostasion*- Arndt-Gingrich defines *apostasion* "A legal t.t. [technical term] found as early as 258 B.C. ... [numerous early usages are cited] in the sense of relinquishment of property after sale, abandonment, etc. the consequent giving up on one's own claim explains the meaning which the word acquires in Jewish circles: (Jer. 3:8) give (one's wife) a certificate of divorce (Matthew 19:7)."[105]

We know the Greek word *apoluo* is equal to the Hebrew word *shalach*, and the Greek word *apostasion* is equal to the Hebrew word *keriythuwth*, because in the marriage passages, when Deuteronomy 24:1 is quoted (Matthew 19:7), the Greek words *apoluo* and *apostasion* are used for the Hebrew words *shalach* and *keriythuwth* respectively. So we do not need a dictionary to tell us the Greek words have the same meaning as the Hebrew words.

Apoluo (Greek) = *shalach* (Hebrew) = put away.

Apostasion (Greek) = *keriythuwth* (Hebrew) = divorcement.

I propose that much of the confusion in regards to what Jesus was referring in the marriage passages is the result of a failure to make a distinction between *apoluo* and *apostasion*. <u>I contend Jesus was referring to the marriage destruction and the practice of certain Jews in the first century who were sending their wives away without giving them a certificate of divorce. I am affirming that the writing of divorcement ends a marriage (i.e. it breaks the bond of marriage), even in the eyes of God! Divorce, by definition, is the opposite of a wedding ceremony.</u>

---

104 Walter Bauer, William F. Arndt, and F. Wilbur Gingrich, *A GREEK ENGLISH LEXICON OF THE NEW TESTAMENT*, 95, 96. (BAG) give some extra-biblical textual examples to support their contention of divorce as a meaning of *apoluo*. Dan Knight, particularly on pages 36-37 in his article "What Jesus Really Said: Putting Away the Mistranslations about Divorce," exposes some weakness of these extra-biblical texts given in support for this word meaning "divorce." As we shall discover, those cultures outside Israel did not give a writing of divorcement; their divorces were verbal i.e. they simply put one another away. The writing of divorcement was unique to Israel.

105 Walter Bauer, William F. Arndt, and F. Wilbur Gingrich, *A GREEK ENGLISH LEXICON OF THE NEW TESTAMENT*, 97.

The latter begins a marriage, the former terminates it.

As with the word "adultery," we shall look at these words and how they are used in scripture to determine their meaning. Most lexicons say "as to divorce" as a meaning of *apoluo*.

David R. Ferguson says in his article "Apoluo Does NOT Mean Divorce":

> Denominationally influenced scholars say apoluo means divorce in some contexts, but that is for you and I to determine.[106]

What does the bible say? That is what we want to know

Isaiah 50:1 **Thus saith Jehovah, Where is the bill of your mother's divorcement, wherewith I have put her away? or which of my creditors is it to whom I have sold you? Behold, for your iniquities were ye sold, and for your transgressions was your mother put away.** (ASV)

"Where is the bill of your mother's divorcement" is a rhetorical question suggesting the answer that Judah had not been given a bill of divorcement, rather she had only been put away.

Jamieson-Fausset-Brown's Commentary:

> VER. 1-11. THE JUDGMENTS ON ISRAEL WERE PROVOKED BY THEIR CRIMES, YET THEY ARE NOT FINALLY CAST OFF BY GOD.. Where . . . mother's divorcement — Zion is "the mother;" the Jews are the children; and God the Husband and Father (ch. 54. 5; 62. 5; Jeremiah 3. 14). GESENIUS thinks, God means by the question to *deny* that He had given "a bill of divorcement" to her, as was often done on slight pretexts by a husband (Deuteronomy 24. 1), or that He had "sold" His and her "children," as a poor parent sometimes did (Exodus 21.7; 2 Kings 4. 1; Nehemiah 5. 5) under pressure of his "creditors;"

---

106 David R., Ferguson "*Apoluo* Does NOT Mean Divorce," article on the totalhealth.bz website. URL: www.totalhealth.bz/divorce-and-remarriage-apoluo.htm (accessed 3/18/17).

that it was they who sold themselves through their own sins. MAURER explains, "*Show* the bill of your mother's divorcement, whom, &c.; produce the creditors to whom ye have been sold ; so it will be seen that it was not from any caprice of mine, but through your own fault, your mother has been put away, and you sold " (ch. 52. 3). HORSLEY best explains (as the antithesis between "I" and "yourselves" shows, though LOWTH translates, *"Ye are sold"*) I have never given your mother a regular bill of divorcement, I have merely "put her away" for a time, and can, therefore, by right as her husband still take her back on her submission; I have not made you, the children, over to any "creditor" to satisfy a debt; I therefore still have the right of a father over you, and can take you back on repentance, though as rebellious children you have sold yourselves to sin and Its penalty (1 Kings 21. 25).[107]

We are told God finally gave Israel a bill of divorcement (Jeremiah 3:8, cf. 2 Kings 17:18), but we do not find where God ever divorced Judah. He put her away (2 Kings 23:27) because of her unfaithfulness and to bring her to repentance, but He did not divorce her. (Isaiah 54:5-10)

Deuteronomy 24:1 **When a man hath taken a wife, and married her, and it come to pass that she find no favour in his eyes, because he hath found some uncleanness in her: then let him write her a bill of divorcement** (*kariythuwth*)**, and give it in her hand, and send** (*shalach*) **her out of his house.**

If *shalach* means "divorce," this is how the passage would read:

Deuteronomy 24:1 **When a man hath taken a wife, and married her, and it come to pass that she find no favour in**

---

107 Robert Jamieson, Andrew Robert Fausset and David Brown, *A COMMENTARY CRITICAL AND EXPLANATORY, ON THE OLD AND NEW TESTAMENTS*, (New York: S.S. Scranton and Company, 1875 [originally published in 1871]), 487 (Google book page number 553). Accessed online via Google Books. URL: https://play.google.com/books/reader?printsec=frontcover&output=reader&id=gMIVAAAAYAA-J&pg=GBS.PA486 (3/18/17).

his eyes, because he hath found some uncleanness in her: then let him write her a bill of divorcement, and give it in her hand, and divorce her.[108]

This translation would have the man divorcing his wife twice! The KJV never translates the word *shalach* "divorce." Strong's does not give "divorce" as a meaning of *shalach*.[109]

Malachi 2:14-16 **Yet ye say, Wherefore? Because the LORD hath been witness between thee and the wife of thy youth, against whom thou hast <u>dealt treacherously: yet is she thy companion, and the wife of thy covenant</u>. And did not he make one? Yet had he the residue of the spirit. And wherefore one? That he might seek a godly seed. Therefore take heed to your spirit, and let none deal treacherously against the wife of his youth. For the LORD, the <u>God of Israel, saith that he hateth putting away</u>: for one covereth violence with his garment, saith the LORD of hosts: therefore take heed to your spirit, that ye deal not treacherously.**[110]

We see from Deuteronomy 24 that God commanded them to write a bill of divorcement, but here we see He hates putting away; therefore, we conclude that the writing of divorcement is not the same as putting away.

Notice also in regards to the man's wife to whom God says the man "has dealt treacherously" is still his wife, that is, she is still "the wife of thy covenant." According to Deuteronomy 24, the woman that is given the writing of divorcement is no longer the man's wife because she may lawfully go and be another man's wife without it being adultery. So we see in Malachi the "put away" (shalach) woman is still the man's wife while the woman given a written bill of divorcement is no longer the man's wife.

Jeremiah 3:8 **And I saw, when for all the causes whereby**

---

108 The wording of this passage has been changed to show what it would say if the word *shalach* was translated "divorce."
109 Strong, STRONG'S EXHAUSTIVE CONCORDANCE OF THE BIBLE, Dictionary of the Hebrew Bible, Dictionary of the Greek Testament, 116.
110 Underlining added for emphasis.

backsliding Israel committed adultery I had put her away, and given her a bill of divorce; yet her treacherous sister Judah feared not, but went and played the harlot also.

Notice God says He did two things; He "put Israel away," which was one thing, and He gave her "a bill of divorcement," which was another thing. Every divorcement involves a putting away, but not every putting away involves a divorcement.

Jesus used a form of *apoluo* eleven times in the marriage passages in Matthew, Mark, and Luke. In every passage He forbade *apoluo*, i.e. putting away. He never forbade giving *apostasion*, i.e. the written divorce, required by Jewish Law.

It is unfortunate many modern speech translations do not make a distinction between *apoluo* and *apostasion* in that they translate *apoluo* as "divorce" in the marriage passages- some every time, and some make one exception:

Matthew 19:7 **They say unto him, Why did Moses then command to give a writing of divorcement** *(apostasion)*, **and to put her away** *(apoluo)*?

Why? Because both words *"apoluo"* and *"apostasion"* occur in this passage.

Translating *apoluo* "divorce" is basically a commentary by the translators. By their translation they have limited the opportunity of the reader to make a determination as to how the word should be understood based on context and exegeses. Of the 63 verses where the word apoluo appears in the KJV translation it is not translated "divorce" but with one exception, Matthew 5:32. Why the translators were inconsistent in this one instance is unknowable, especially since the same word *apoluo* appears twice in this verse and once in the previous verse and was translated "put away" two out of the three times. However, this one unfortunate instance may be the source of the confusion. The translators of the American Standard Version corrected this translation, but the ASV never achieved the popularity of the KJV. The KJV is still the most popular and has always been the most influential English translation. The ASV consistently and correctly translates apoluo "put away" in the marriage passages.

In an article by Chuck Winters, Biblical Misconceptions about Divorce and Remarriage (The Church Shooting Her Wounded) he says:

> Now, we are going to add to our general lack of understanding of ancient Hebrew customs and attitudes toward women. Much of our current confusion over the issue of divorce and remarriage began when the translators of the English Bible began to translate these two very different words in both the Hebrew Old Testament and the Greek New Testament with the one word **divorce**.
>
> Jerome in his Latin Vulgate never did this. This was never done in the Aramaic versions. This was never done in Martin Luther's German translation. For the first 1,500 years of our Bible's translation history all translators kept these 2 words and their meanings distinct. The same was true of the Septuagint's Greek translation of the Old Testament.
>
> For English Bible translators to equate **putting away** with **divorce**, with our modern day understanding of social values that see women as something other than the property of men, has led to tremendous confusion.[111]

The Greek word *apoluo* meant dismissal by the husband and may or may not have included a writing of divorce. *Apostasion* was specific; it did include a writing of divorce. It is my conviction *apoluo* refers to the marriage destruction, not the divorce certificate that ends the marriage officially. Jesus was also addressing the continuing practice of certain Jews in the

---

[111] Chuck Winters, "Biblical Misconceptions about Divorce and Remarriage (The Church Shooting Her Wounded)," paper found on the *brutallyhonest.org* website. URL: http://www.brutallyhonest.org/brutally_honest/files/Biblical%20Misconceptions%20About%20Divorce%20and%20Remarriage.pdf (accessed 7/7/17), 10.

first century who were sending their wives away, breaking their marriage covenant, often without giving them a certificate of divorce. The breaking of the marriage covenant and the heartless practice of withholding the divorce certificate was what Jesus was referring to in the Sermon on the Mount, and His words against this practice were the motive behind the question of the Pharisees in Matthew 19.

Walter Callison, in his book *DIVORCE: A GIFT OF GOD'S LOVE*, writes:

> *"Apoluo"* the Greek word for putting away, was not technically divorce, though often used synonymously. In that time of total male domination, men often took additional wives and did not provide a written release when they forsook wives and married others. The law demanding written divorce (Deut. 24:1, 2) was largely ignored... The distinction between *"put away"* and *"divorce,"* between the Greek *"apoluo"* and *"apostasion"* is critical. *"Apoluo"* indicated that women were enslaved, put away, with no rights, no recourse; deprived of the basic right to a monogamous marriage. *"Apostasion"* ended marriage and permitted a legal subsequent marriage. The paper makes a difference... Maybe large numbers of common men didn't customarily put aside their wives or take additional wives without giving written divorce, but we have plenty of evidence of disregard for the rights of women and proof that some did, indicating the likelihood that this was the problem Jesus was addressing when he said "whosoever putteth away his wife..."(Luke 16:18)... Oral divorce come under the meaning of the word *apoluo,* failure to observe the nicety of a writing of divorcement.[112]

Josephus says in Antiquities of the Jews:

> He that desires to be divorced from his wife for any cause whatsoever (and many such causes happen

---
112 Walter Callison, *DIVORCE: A GIFT OF GOD'S LOVE* (Leawood, KS: Leathers Publishing, 2002), 5, 42.

> among men), let him in writing give assurance that he will never use her as his wife any more; for by this means she may be at liberty to marry another husband, although before this bill of divorce be given, she is not permitted so to do...[113]

Part of the problem in distinguishing "put away" from "divorcement" is the fact that in nations outside of Israel and those cultures surrounding Israel divorce was accomplished by simply putting away without the requirement of a certificate of divorce.

David Amram says:

> The Bill of Divorce Peculiarly A Jewish Form of Separation-The giving of a Bill of Divorce to a wife was a custom peculiar to the Hebrews, and the heathen nations round about the Jews did not give Bills of Divorce to their wives when they sent them away. Rabbi Yohanan (199-279 C. E.) states that the heathen gave no Bill of Divorce when they sent away their wives; they simply divorced each other by separating without formality.[114]

During the time of Moses, the law most accepted by the surrounding heathen societies was the Hammurabi law code. Hammurabi, ruler of Babylon, reigned from 1795 to 1750 BC. The Law code of Hammurabi has been translated into English by L.W. King and is available online. Law codes 133-149 basically deal with marriage and divorce.[115] The formal divorce was oral and involved money compensation, and the informal was desertion. Women could also divorce men under certain circumstances.

---

113 Flavius Josephus, *THE ANTIQUITIES OF THE JEWS*, contained within *THE WORKS OF JOSEPHUS: Complete and Unabridged*, translated by William Whiston, NEW UPDATED EDITION, (Peabody, MA: Hendrickson Publishers, 2008), Book 4, Chapter 8, 120.
114 David Amram, *THE JEWISH LAW OF DIVORCE according to the Bible and the Talmund with Some References to its Development in Post-Talmudic Times*, (New York, NY: Harmon Press, 1968 [originally published in 1896]), 135.
115 Hammurabi, "The Code of Hammurabi," translated by L.W. King, found online at the Yale Law School Avalon Project website, URL: http://avalon.law.yale.edu/ancient/hamframe.asp (accessed 3/25/17).

During the time of Christ, the surrounding societies consisted of the Romans and the Greeks.

David Amram says:

> Form of Divorce Among the Greeks and Romans-Among the Greeks as well as the Romans either the husband or the wife could divorce the other. Technically the divorce of the wife by the husband was "αποπομπη" (sending away) and the divorce of the husband by the wife "απολευψις" (leaving). The woman could not send away her husband because she had been brought into his house from which she could not, of course eject him, but she could *leave* his house and go back to her kin. The free marriage could be easily dissolved by either party... The divorce was usually accompanied by some act indicative of the separation, such as giving back the dowry, taking away the keys from the wife and the like... The Bill of Divorce was not introduced at Rome... until the reign of Diocletian (284-305 C.E.).[116]

It would be naive to think the surrounding cultures did not have some influence on the Jewish people in Moses' day as well as in the days of Christ's earthly ministry. Just as our surrounding culture influences Christians today, we can be sure the Jews of old were not exempt from such influences because human nature has remained consistent through the ages.

Walter Callison says:

> The Jewish law demanding written divorce (Deut. 24:1-2) could be ignored without social stigma or legal recourse... If a man married another woman so what? If a man "put away "(*apoluo*)" his wife without bothering with a divorce ("get") who was going to object? The woman?[117]

It seems obvious from the exchange Jesus had with the Phari-

---
116 Amram, *THE JEWISH LAW OF DIVORCE*, 138, 139.
117 Callison, *DIVORCE: A GIFT OF GOD'S LOVE*, 43.

sees in Mark chapter ten that the Pharisees considered the writing of divorcement an option that could be ignored. The fact Jesus used the word "command" and the Pharisees changed the thrust of Jesus' question about a command to answer with what they perceived as a liberty is telling.

Mark 10:3-5 **And he answered and said unto them, What did Moses command you? And they said, Moses suffered to write a bill of divorcement, and to put her away. 5 And Jesus answered and said unto them, For the hardness of your heart he wrote you this precept**("command" -ASV).

The word "suffered" is Strong's #2010 "epitrepw epitrepo, ep-ee-trep'-o from 1909 and the base of 5157; to turn over (transfer), i.e. allow:--give leave (liberty, license), let, permit, suffer."[118]

In Mark's account, Jesus says the writing of divorcement was a command, but notice what Jesus says in Matthew's account about a "putting away" passage.

Matthew 19:8 **He saith unto them, Moses because of the hardness of your hearts suffered you to put away your wives: but from the beginning it was not so.**

If "put away" means "divorce," then we have Moses permitting something and at the same time commanding it.

I believe "putting away" (often without the certificate of divorce) is the issue in dispute between Jesus and the Pharisees. In the next chapter, we shall examine the exchange between Jesus and the Jewish leaders of His day and see if we can get to the bottom of the marriage and divorce issue.

---

118 Strong, *STRONG'S EXHAUSTIVE CONCORDANCE OF THE BIBLE, Dictionary of the Hebrew Bible, Dictionary of the Greek Testament*, 32.

CHAPTER VII: MATTHEW 19:3-9

Matthew 19:5-6 **And said, For this cause shall a man leave father and mother, and shall cleave to his wife: and they twain shall be one flesh? Wherefore they are no more twain, but one flesh. What therefore God hath joined together, <u>let not man put asunder</u>.**[119]

1 Timothy 4:1-3 **Now the Spirit speaketh expressly, that in the latter times some shall depart from the faith, giving heed to seducing spirits, and <u>doctrines of devils</u>; Speaking lies in hypocrisy; having their conscience seared with a hot iron; <u>Forbidding to marry</u>.**[120]

God is against marriage-breaking and for marriage-making.

Z.T. Sweeney says:

> Let both writer and reader therefore cast aside any flippancy of spirit, also any preconceptions or prejudices, and say like young Samuel of old: "Speak, Lord; thy servant heareth." The subject may be made plain or simple according to the manner we may treat it.[121]

So let us now take a look and see what Jesus really said in the marriage passages. We shall use as our core text Matthew 19:3-12, but we shall also examine the other marriage texts as we go along because they will supply additional information and insight not revealed in Matthew 19.

Matthew 19:3-9 **The Pharisees also came unto him, tempting him, and saying unto him, Is it lawful for a man to put**

---
[119] Underlining added for emphasis.
[120] Ibid.
[121] Zachary Taylor Sweeney, The Spirit and the Word: A Treatise on the Holy Spirit in the Light of a Rational Interpretation of the Word of Truth, (Nashville, TN: The Gospel Advocate Company, 1875 [this may be the original publication date]). The edition quoted is the 2005 e-book from Project Gutenberg's e-book collection. Accessed online via gutenberg.org. URL: http://www.gutenberg.org/cache/epub/15011/pg15011.txt (accessed 4/14/17), the quote is from the introduction which evidently originally started on page 5 and ended on page 8.

away his wife for every cause? And he answered and said unto them, Have ye not read, that he which made them at the beginning made them male and female, And said, For this cause shall a man leave father and mother, and shall cleave to his wife: and they twain shall be one flesh? Wherefore they are no more twain, but one flesh. What therefore God hath joined together, let not man put asunder. They say unto him, Why did Moses then command to give a writing of divorcement, and to put her away? He saith unto them, Moses because of the hardness of your hearts suffered you to put away your wives: but from the beginning it was not so. And I say unto you, Whosoever shall put away his wife, except it be for fornication, and shall marry another, committeth adultery: and whoso marrieth her which is put away doth commit adultery.**

So let us break this down and see what is being said in these passages.

Matthew 19:3 **The Pharisees also came unto him, tempting him, and saying unto him, Is it lawful for a man to put away his wife for every cause?**

The question is not: *Is it lawful for a man to marry after divorce?*

The question is: *Is it lawful for a man to put away his wife for every cause?*

Notice this was a test question i.e. they were "trying Him." Many believe the test was concerning the heated debate between the schools of Shammai and Hillel because of the "for every cause" portion of the question. Basically, the school of Rabbi Hillel took the liberal interpretation that a man could divorce his wife for any displeasure he had with her, whereas, the school of Rabbi Shammai took the stricter interpretation-only moral transgressions are legitimate grounds to divorce a wife. Why would this question be a test for Jesus? If Jesus took the side of the Pharisees who identified with the school of Hillel, or the Sadducees who identified with the school of Shammai, it would put Him in either one Jewish camp or the other. Another problem with this supposed question is the fact neither school forbade divorce for any cause in practice.

David Instone-Brewer says:

> Even after a Hilleite "any matter" divorce. They [the Shammaites] decided that if a legal court granted a divorce, they would not countermand the court's decision even though it was counter to what they could have decided.[122]

I do not believe the question was concerning the debate about the legality of divorce between the two rabbinical schools since both schools agreed that divorce ended the marriage and was lawful (because it was lawful according to Deuteronomy 24:1- this would not have been denied by any Jew, or Jesus, for that matter, even those of the school of Shammai). I believe the question was about the practice of sending a wife away, often without a divorce certificate. Notice in the text the word "divorce" is not actually mentioned until verse 7. The question was, <u>Is it lawful to put away one's wife</u>, that is, to send her away? ("for every cause" was an attempt to disguise it as a legitimate question). Notice in Marks account:

Mark 10:2 **And the Pharisees came to him, and asked him, Is it lawful for a man to put away his wife? tempting him.**

There is no mention of "for every cause" here, just the question, "is it lawful to put away one's wife." I believe the trap was in the fact the Jews interpreted Moses to say in Deuteronomy 24:1 God approves of a man putting away his wife and their question presupposes knowledge of Jesus' position on the matter. The Jews had heard or were present when Jesus made His statement about "putting away" in the Sermon on the Mount. They believed Jesus' position contradicted the Law. They wanted to expose Jesus as one who was opposed

---

[122] David Instone-Brewer, *DIVORCE AND REMARRIAGE IN THE BIBLE*, (Grand Rapids, MI: Wm. B. Eerdmans, 2002), 167.

to Moses' Law. So let us go to the Sermon on the Mount and examine what Jesus said.

Matthew 5:31-32 It hath been said, Whosoever shall put away his wife, let him give her a writing of divorcement: 32 But I say unto you, That whosoever shall put away his wife, saving for the cause of fornication, causeth her to commit adultery: and whosoever shall marry her that is divorced committeth adultery.

Notice Jesus did not say "it is written"; rather, He says "it hath been said." Jesus is not referring to what is written in the Law, but what is being said about what is written in the Law. The question for us is *Who said it and what were they saying?* The Jewish leaders of Jesus' day (who considered themselves caretakers of God's law and their interpretation to be the law itself) were justifying themselves in putting away their wives (breaking their marriage covenants), often without divorce by their misinterpretation of Deuteronomy 24:1. They claimed Moses was approving the action of putting away even without the certificate. We see this from their reaction to Jesus' statement in Matthew 19:6 **Wherefore they are no more twain, but one flesh. What therefore God hath joined together, <u>let not man put asunder</u>.**[123] Remember in a previous section we discovered the Greek meant Jesus was saying "you are sundering your marriages and I am ordering you to stop." The Pharisees gave the following response found in Matthew 19:7: **They say unto him, Why did Moses then command to give a writing of divorcement, <u>and to put her away</u>?**[124] The expression "and to put her away" indicates they thought God, through Moses, was approving the action of putting away. "Why else would God instruct them to give a writing of divorcement if God did not approve of putting their wives away?" was how they were reasoning. They thought Moses said "Okay men, go ahead and put away your wives." Jesus' statement in the Sermon on the Mount contradicted their supposed provision from God.

---

123 Underlining added for emphasis.
124 Ibid.

Matthew 5:32 **but I say unto you, that every one that putteth away his wife, saving for the cause of fornication, maketh her an adulteress: and whosoever shall marry her when she is put away committeth adultery.** (ASV) What Jesus says here is the man who puts away a legitimate and innocent wife "makes her an adulteress." It is possible the KJV does not render this passage properly because the word for "adulteress" in this passage is in the passive voice in the Greek, meaning the woman is being made an adulteress; not that she is committing adultery. This is evident from the fact a woman who did not remarry would not commit adultery and it would not be true as Jesus says "every one that putteth away his wife, maketh her an adulteress." Jesus is pointing the finger of blame at the man, not the woman. The man, by his actions, is making this woman an adulteress when she is not. This is evident by the fact Jesus used the word *"Poiei."* (to make, cause, to bring about)[125] That is, this man is making an innocent, legitimate wife appear to be the guilty one when she is not. How can that be (would be the thinking of the Pharisee) since God permits putting away? And then Jesus goes on to say that if a man puts away a legitimate wife and she were to marry another, then the man marrying her would commit adultery. Why? Because she is still married to her first husband. He has put her away, but without a writing of divorcement. R.C.H. Lenski, in his commentary on Matthew, says "He brings about that she is stigmatized as adulterous" and then adds in the second sentence of the verse "he [the man marrying the put away woman] is stigmatized as adulterous." He (Lenski) thinks the man marrying the "put away" woman is also stigmatized as adulterous, which is certainly plausible. Some have suggested Jesus is anticipating this woman marrying another man after divorce because of the second clause of this passage.

Lenski says:

> Some commentators are "under the influence of the traditional exegesis" when considering this verse, without realizing it, and that is the basis of their the-

---
125 see Walter Bauer, William F. Arndt, and F. Wilbur Gingrich, A GREEK ENGLISH LEXICON OF THE NEW TESTAMENT 688.

ory, not the words of the text... This theory makes the agent of *moicheuthenai* the man mentioned in the next sentence who later may marry this wronged woman. This is grammatically untenable. The agent of a passive infinitive or of an active infinitive cannot be introduced from a sentence that follows.[126]

Frank Stagg, in THE BROADMAN BIBLE COMMENTARY, says:

> The Greek text does not justify the translation "causeth her to commit adultery (KJV)." The infinitive is passive (*moicheuthenai*), untranslatable in English. Something like "made adulterous" or "victimized with respect to adultery" approaches the idea. The RSV is little improvement over the KJV here. We know nothing about Jesus which would justify understanding him to say that an innocent wife-is an adulteress because her husband divorces her.[127]

Jesus is saying the man putting away his wife is responsible for making or branding a legitimate wife an "adulteress,"[128] and is also an accessory to the adultery of the man who marries her, because she has been put away, not legitimately divorced. Again (according to the Jews) how can that be if God approves of them putting away their wives?

The Jews of Jesus' day thought God through Moses approved of them putting away their wives with or without a writing of divorcement and thought Jesus was in conflict with the Law on this matter. Remember, the Jewish leaders thought the writing of divorcement was optional and could be ignored. We learn this from Mark 10:4 **And they said, Moses <u>suffered</u> to write**

---

126 Lenski, THE INTERPRETATION OF ST. MATHEW'S GOSPEL, 232.
127 Frank Stagg, *THE BROADMAN BIBLE COMMENTARY*, (Nashville, TN: Broadman Press, 1969), Volume 8, Matthew, 110.
128 John Murray says: "While it is true some kind of passive force may have to be recognized, the passive cannot be forced into this kind of service. The idea of merely subjective judgment on part of others is not inherent in the passive. And whatever strength may be given to the passive in this case, the woman is still viewed as implicated in adultery." John Murray, *DIVORCE*, (Phillipsburg, NJ: Presbyterian and Reformed Publishing Co., 1961), 24. Whether John Murray is correct or not, it cannot be denied the husband putting away his wife is the one being held accountable for the adultery of the wife in this passage, because she is put away, not divorced.

a bill of divorcement, and to put her away.[129] Jesus responds by saying God has at no time approved of marriage-breaking: "let not man put asunder." This statement shows that God had not, through Moses, changed His position in regards to marriage. Jesus is, in essence, saying God has never approved of marriage-breaking. Let me say that it is interesting that the traditional view makes the same misinterpretation of Moses as the Pharisees. They say God had a strict marriage and divorce law and then Moses loosened the Law and allowed marriage-breaking for about any reason under the sun, and then Jesus comes along and changed the law and restored it to God's original intent, except in the case of adultery. This, in my opinion, paints God as fickle and indecisive. The fact that Jesus said "let not man put asunder," which in the Greek construction is a present imperative with a negative particle *me*, means Jesus was saying "you are sundering your marriages and it is wrong (Why? Because it has always been wrong, even from the beginning.), and I am ordering you to stop." He was not talking to people in the future directly; He was directing this statement to these Pharisees. This shows that Moses did not say it was okay to break one's marriage, as the Pharisees and those who hold the traditional view claim. This also shows God has been consistent through time in regards to marriage and marriage-breaking.

Jesus' response to the first question asked in verse three was the response the Pharisees had anticipated, or at least something along the same line. The question in verse three was given because they already knew Jesus' position on the matter and it was given to set Jesus up for the next question.

Matthew 19:7 **They say unto him, Why did Moses then command to give a writing of divorcement, and to put her away?**

This is the question they wanted to get to and ask, and this is the test Matthew refers to in verse three. They thought they had Jesus in a position to expose Him as being in opposition

---
129 Underlining added for emphasis.

to Moses and the Law. If Jesus is right, then Moses must be wrong (which would be an unacceptable conclusion), and if Moses is right, then Jesus must be wrong and could be condemned as a false prophet.

Olan Hicks says:

> Of course Moses had not commanded men to put away their wives. They were already doing that. What he did command was that in the case where a wife was being put away the man must give her a written bill of divorce and that he was never to take her again as his wife after she had been married to another man (Deuteronomy 24:1-4). The gist of the Pharisees' question was why would Moses legislate a bill of divorcement procedure if God does not approve of men putting away their wives?[130]

Jesus' answer:

Matthew 19:8 **He saith unto them, Moses because of the hardness of your hearts suffered you to put away your wives: but from the beginning it was not so.**[131]

Jesus was saying: God did not give the writing of divorcement because He approved of you putting away your wives, but because you were already putting away your wives, and because of the cruel and hardhearted way you were doing it, that is, without a writing of divorcement, so that she may go be another man's wife. Not all men were hardhearted; there were those who put away their wives and gave them a writing of divorcement, which was the humane thing to do. However, there were men who were callous and uncaring in that they were not concerned with the plight of the wives they were putting away; their only concern was themselves. Therefore, God had to command these hardhearted men to give their wives a writing of divorcement when they put them away, but it was not because He approved of "putting away," but as a means of rescue for these women. Jesus' explanation of what God

---
130 Hicks, *WHAT THE BIBLE SAYS ABOUT MARRIAGE, DIVORCE, & REMARRIAGE*, 63.
131 Underlining added for emphasis.

commanded concerning the "bill of divorcement" is this: if you are going to put away your wife (i.e. repudiate her), set her free; put in her hand a bill of divorcement. This was important because women did not have the same rights as men in regards to marriage and especially divorce. The woman could not divorce her husband. This is not stated specifically in the Law, but David Amram says:

> The reason for silence of the law on this question is, however, obvious. In a state of society where the husband and father was practically a sovereign in dealing with his own, the case of a wife suing for divorce could not have occurred to the lawgivers, because there was no forum in which she could obtain redress. The wife was part of the husband's *familia*, and looked to her lord and master for her law.[132]

Paul, in his letter to the Romans, confirms this fact in regards to women not being able to sue for divorce under the law. Romans 7:1-4 **Or are ye ignorant, brethren (for I speak to men who know the law), that the law hath dominion over a man for so long time as he liveth? 2 <u>For the woman that hath a husband is bound by law to the husband while he liveth; but if the husband die, she is discharged from the law of the husband</u>. 3 So then if, while the husband liveth, she be joined to another man, she shall be called an adulteress: but if the husband die, she is free from the law, so that she is no adulteress, though she be joined to another man. 4 Wherefore, my brethren, ye also were made dead to the law through the body of Christ; that ye should be joined to another, even to him who was raised from the dead, that we might bring forth fruit unto God.**[133]

The woman according to Jewish law could not divorce her husband; therefore, as far as she was concerned, once she married a man she was bound to him until his death.[134] This was not the

---
132 Amram, *THE JEWISH LAW OF DIVORCE*, 54.
133 Underlining added for emphasis.
134 The woman not being allowed to divorce her husband was not a moral issue, but a legal

case for the man under the law, as Deuteronomy 24:1 clearly states. That is why Paul used the illustration of the woman[135] under the law, and not the man, because the man would not fit. It is unfortunate that some in the church have tried to take Paul's illustration and apply it to both men and women, disregarding the fact that this is an illustration of the woman under the law and then trying to make a New Testament application of it. By doing so, they not only destroy the meaning of the passage, but make a very destructive application of these passages in regards to those who have been divorced. The woman under the law was a perfect parallel to the situation of the Jew in terms of the Law of Moses and Christ. The woman could not divorce her husband under Jewish law;[136] she was bound until death. Likewise the Jewish people could not divorce God; they were bound to the law until death. The man under the law was not so bound and would not have been suitable as an illustration. Also, the woman could not have more than one husband because she could not be under the law of two husbands at a time, there again making a perfect illustration to the situation of the Jews. Just like the woman under the law, the Jewish people could not be under two laws at the same time (i.e. the Law of Moses and the law of Christ). This would not be true for the man under the law because it was lawful for him to have more than one wife at a time and he was never under the law of his wife. He was never in subjection to her, nor did he have to wait for her to die to be released from the law of his wife because he was never under such a law! The woman, by virtue of the death of her husband, was released from the law of her husband and could marry another. In like figure the Jews, because of the death of Jesus, could by virtue of His death be married to Him. To apply this passage as a marriage law in

---

one. Women were not allowed to divorce their husbands because they had no legal provision to do so, not because it was immoral. If it was morally wrong, it would be just as wrong for the man as the woman. A perfect example is that found in the early history of America. Between 1776 and 1920 women in America were not allowed to vote, not because their voting was immoral but because they had no legal provision to do so. The prohibition was based on culturally accepted norms of the time.

135 The Greek word for "wife," *gune*, occurs about 200 times in the New Testament and not once is it used in a generic sense (i.e. referring to both men and women). It always refers specifically to mature females.

136 There is indication in Paul's letter to the Corinthians (chapter seven) that women could divorce their husbands under the New Testament. We shall explore this when we look into marriage in the New Testament.

the New Testament is taking Paul's illustration out of context and grossly misapplying it. But the point we want to make is, if a man puts away his wife and does not give her a writing of divorcement, he puts her in a very precarious situation.

Walter Callison says:

> Marriage was more than a privilege, yes more than a right, to those women. Marriage could mean the difference between life and death. To be put out could be to receive a sentence of starvation or of a life supported by adultery... divorce provided a corrective for an intolerable situation.[137]

A "put away" woman could not get a job as a waitress or the like; she had very few choices, harlotry perhaps, or marrying another man unlawfully, as they sometimes did. The writing of divorcement was given as a means of recovery for the woman in the event she was put away by her husband. God commanding the writing of divorcement in the case of a certain wrong thing that was being done (i.e. putting away one's wife) is not to be understood as approval of the wrong thing. Many of the laws of Moses were of this nature (e.g. Exodus 21:18-19). This hard-hearted practice of putting away without the writing of divorcement was happening during the days of Moses and during the days of Christ's ministry and is still happening today among Orthodox Jews.

Consider this excerpt from a November 12, 2013 article in *Newsweek:* "DIVORCE IN THE ORTHODOX COMMUNITY CAN BE BRUTAL, DEGRADING AND ENDLESS."

> According to Jewish law, a wife can refuse to accept a divorce initiated by her husband, but only a husband can initiate and finalize religious divorce proceedings. Even if a woman obtains a civil divorce, she is not considered divorced under Jewish law until her husband issues a get. Without it, she is deemed an *agunah*, a "chained wife" — she can-

---

137 Callison, *DIVORCE: A GIFT OF GOD'S LOVE*, 67.

not date or remarry within the religious community in which she was raised, and any children she has with a new husband are deemed illegitimate. While a wife can sue for divorce in a *beth din*, a Jewish court, and while the *beth din* can order the husband to issue the get, he can still refuse. For some *agunot*, the situation can become so dire that they turn to violence. Recently, the FBI arrested a group of Brooklyn rabbis for running a for-hire torture ring that kidnapped and tormented Jewish husbands unwilling to provide their wives with gets.

"Being an *agunah* is such a painful and shameful existence," says Fraidy Reiss, founder and executive director of Unchained At Last, a nonprofit that provides free legal services and support to women of any culture or religion trying to leave arranged or forced marriages. "You remain trapped as a single person in a community where there is nothing more shameful than being single."

While there are plenty of cases in which Orthodox Jewish couples divorce without incident, for some husbands, refusing to offer a get is a way to control their wives — to extort money, to blackmail them for custody over children or, more simply, to punish them for wanting to end the marriage...

"Get refusal is a form of domestic abuse, and domestic abuse is never justified," says Rabbi Jeremy Stern, executive director of the Organization for the Resolution of Agunot (ORA), a nonprofit in New York that helps husbands and wives secure gets amicably.[138]

If you search for *"agunah"* on the internet, you will find an amazing amount of information about these "chained women." You will find documentation of this practice all the way back to Moses and all the way to the present day among the

---

138 Abigail Jones, "DIVORCE IN THE ORTHODOX COMMUNITY CAN BE BRUTAL, DEGRADING AND ENDLESS," article in Newsweek, November 12, 2013. Accessed online at URL: http://www.newsweek.com/divorce-orthodox-jewish-community-can-be-brutal-degrading-and-endless-3082 (accessed 5/10/17).

Jews.

God gave the command to give a writing of divorcement to provide a remedy to the hard-hearted practice of some men who were putting away their wives and abandoning them, and in some cases, if they so desired, taking them back again; the woman was helpless in this matter.

Olan Hicks says:

> When God stipulated that in the event of a wife being dismissed the man is to give her a written decree which releases her to marry again, this does not constitute God's approval of marriage breaking. The longsuffering forbearance of God with man's misconduct is one thing. Suggesting the stamp of God's approval upon it is something else.[139]

This is what Jesus meant when He said in Matthew 19:8b: ... **Moses for your hardness of heart <u>suffered</u> you to put away your wives...** (ASV)[140]

What does it mean he "suffered you to put away your wives"? It simply means God did not police putting away or mete out punishment. Consider what would happen if every separation required immediate punishment and divorce. This would lessen, nay *impede*, the possibility of reconciliation, which would be the better option. If something can be done to restore the relationship, of course, every option should be explored before divorce; this is the advice given in 1 Corinthians 7:11: **(but should she depart, let her remain unmarried, or else be reconciled to her husband); and that the husband leave not his wife.** (c.f. Romans 10:21; 9:22-24)

True repentance and forgiveness has restored some of the most traumatized marital relationships imaginable even from the very brink of death. Every effort should be exhausted in order to salvage a broken marriage, but when a marriage is dead, do the paper work; this allows the people involved to be

---
[139] Hicks, *WHAT THE BIBLE SAYS ABOUT MARRIAGE, DIVORCE, & REMARRIAGE*, 17.
[140] Underlining added for emphasis.

free to get on with their lives. This was the very reason God gave the writing of divorcement, i.e., to provide a means of recovery for those Jewish women of Moses' day. The writing of divorcement would serve the same purpose today. It is not the writing of divorcement that breaks the marriage. <u>The one who destroys the relationship and refuses to repair it is the one who breaks the marriage</u>. The problem in Jesus' day was if a man discarded his first wife and took a second wife, there was very little incentive to reconcile with the first wife. The discarding of the first wife and the taking of a second wife was an indication he was done with the first wife. Moses said if a man is going to put away his wife (i.e discard her), then he must put her away with a writing of divorcement. Not because God approved of putting away, but for the sake of the abandoned wife He required it.

God is opposed to marriage-breaking whether by the husband or by the wife. Sometimes (without being given a divorce) the wife would leave her husband and marry another.

Mark 10:12 **and if she herself shall put away her husband, and marry another, she committeth adultery.** (ASV)

God is opposed to marriage-breaking; He is today, He was in the days of Jesus ministry, and He has always been opposed to marriage-breaking.

Matthew 19:8 **8 He saith unto them, Moses for your hardness of heart suffered you to put away your wives: <u>but from the beginning it hath not been so</u>.** (ASV)[141] It has never been so!

So why would a man, any man, put away his wife rather than divorce her; why not just marry another woman and keep them both? Not all men abandoned their wives when they married others. Solomon had 700 wives and 300 concubines, but not once do we hear of him putting away any one of his wives. In fact, if you read the Song of Solomon, a story I believe is

---

141 Underlining added for emphasis.

about Solomon (i.e. "her beloved") and his wife, you will see he knew how to treat a lady. So why would a man, any man, put away his wife rather than divorce her? Let me propose some possible reasons.

First: It may be because the man perceives her as shaming him or deems her as being unpresentable. This is what is indicated by the Hebrew word *ervah* (uncleaness,) in Deuteronomy 24.

In the Greek Septuagint, the Hebrew word erva is translated *aschemon* (Strong's #809).[142] This word is found in 1 Corinthians 12:23: **And those members of the body, which we think to be less honourable, upon these we bestow more abundant honour; and our uncomely** (*aschemon*) **parts have more abundant comeliness.** Bauer, Arndt, and Gingrich define this word as: "shameful, unpresentable, indecent, the unpresentable, i.e. private, parts."[143] A couple of other translations give some insight into the meaning of this word. 1 Corinthians 12:23 **And to those parts of the body which seem to have less honour we give all the more honour; and to those parts of the body which are a cause of shame to us we give the greater respect;** (BBE) and 1 Corinthians 12:23 **And those members of the body which we think to be less honorable, on these we bestow greater honor; and our unpresentable parts have greater modesty,** (WEB)[144]

Second: It may be to keep her under his control to be available if needed or wanted again. This may be the reason for God commanding the husband giving a writing of divorcement and forbidding his remarrying the woman after she has been made another man's wife (Deuteronomy 24:3-4).

Let me give an overview of the times that led up to this exchange Jesus had with these Pharisees. In the early history of

---

142 This word is used in the Septuagint (LXX) version of the Old Testament in Deuteronomy 24:1. A copy of the Septuagint can be found at URL: http://www.septuagint.org/LXX/?ac=1 (accessed 7/8/17). Another version, based on the Septuagint, edited by Alfred Rahlfs, Second Revised Edition, edited by Robert Hanhart, can be found at URL: https://www.academic-bible.com/en/online-bibles/septuagint-lxx/read-the-bible-text/ (accessed 7/8/17). The online edition is claimed to be copyrighted © 2006 Deutsche Bibelgesellschaft, Stuttgart.
143 Walter Bauer, William F. Arndt, and F. Wilbur Gingrich, *A GREEK ENGLISH LEXICON OF THE NEW TESTAMENT*, 119.
144 For these two passages, underlining was added for emphasis.

mankind all divorces were verbal. Even those among God's people; for example, when Abraham divorced Hagar, he simply sent her away or put her away (Genesis 21:10-14). This was the custom among all people; however, when we come to the time of Moses, there was an abuse of this practice that God dealt with in the law. What some men began to do was put away their wives, and then when she would seek another man to marry, her former husband would recant and claim he never divorced her, placing her in a position of committing adultery (as well as her second husband) because she would be married to two husbands (c.f. Romans 7:3). The problem with this custom was it often left the women in a state of not being officially divorced while not being married in practice. She then was left with few options to fend for herself. To correct this abuse, God commanded the writing of divorcement be given in the event a man puts away his wife. In that case, if the man tries to claim he did not divorce her, she could produce the proof because she would have, in her hand, an official document declaring her to be divorced from her husband. This would free her and allow her to marry another, thus providing a means of protection and recovery for these Israelite women. When we come to Jesus' day, we find that certain men found a way to continue this evil practice by simply putting away their wives but not giving them a writing of divorcement. They were abandoning them, putting them out, and bringing in another woman. They actually justified this practice through their twisting of God's law in Deuteronomy 24, claiming God allowed them to put away their wives and the writing of divorcement was optional. So they took the law that was given to prevent such practice and turned it on its head and used it to authorize the very thing the law was meant to prevent.

Third: It could have been a situation of jealousy, spite, and control by not allowing the woman to be another man's wife. This is still occurring today among Orthodox Jews. Notice this excerpt from a New York Post article from November 4, 2013 titled "An orthodox woman's 3-year divorce fight."

> Few people outside the tight-knit Orthodox Jewish community have heard of the get — the crucial document in Jewish law which a husband must sign before a divorce is finalized in the eyes of God.
>
> Without it, the wife, known as an agunah, is not allowed to marry again. If she has children, they are considered bastards. The man, however, can move on without a get, openly dating other women.
>
> The contentious issue of the get came to public notice last month after two rabbis in Brooklyn were accused of charging vulnerable agunot up to $60,000 each to kidnap and torture husbands who refused to sign the paperwork.
>
> ... "The refusal to issue a get is never justified and is defined in Jewish law as domestic abuse," says Rabbi Jeremy Stern, executive director of ORA.
>
> Some agunot have been waiting as long as 10 years after their marriages ended in the civil courts. Others have been unable to unchain themselves from husbands who are criminals or even pedophiles.
>
> "<u>It's the last form of control the husband has over his wife,</u>" adds Stern. "<u>The mentality is, 'If I can't have her, no one can.' It's fundamentally about control and spite.</u>"[145]

Fourth: The biggest factor, and most likely reason, is pure greed i.e. money. In this respect, it is important that we have a clear understanding of Jewish law as it pertains to the dowry. To help understand, let us observe the explanation given by David Amram in his book <u>The Jewish Law of Divorce</u>:

> The husband would certainly not go through the unpleasant formalities of a public accusation of his wife, if he could without question, rid himself of her by a Bill of Divorce. The answer to this is

---

145 Doree Lewak, "An orthodox woman's 3 year divorce fight," 11/4/2013, article on the New York Post website under the Living section. URL: http://nypost.com/2013/11/04/orthodox-jewish-womans-plea-for-a-divorce/ (accessed 6/2/17). Underlining added for emphasis.

found in the law of the wife's dowry. By a contract, expressed or implied, the husband secured to his wife, in the event of his death or divorce, a certain sum of money, and also, by later law, the return to her of the property which she brought to him upon her marriage. If the wife was found guilty of ante-nuptial incontinence, she was put to death; but if the husband divorced her without public inquiry, she was entitled to her dowry and to the return of the property which was brought to her husband at her marriage... In all cases where the husband refused to pay his wife the amount of the Kethubah, she had the right of appeal to the courts, who heard and determined the merits of the case. If the decision was against the husband and he failed to pay, his lands and goods could be attached and sold by order of the court at public sale for the purpose of satisfying her claim. If the estate of the husband was insufficient they proceeded against the estate formerly in his possession, and which was now in the hands of third persons, and until the last perutah of her dowry was paid, her husband was obliged to support her... After the divorce, the separation of the husband and wife was absolute. His power over her and his rights in her estate, her earnings, etc., were at an end, although she still had certain rights against him. Until he had paid her dowry in full she was entitled to be supported by him as though she was still his wife.[146]

As you can see, it would be advantageous to simply put away one's wife without the formal divorce, thereby retaining the dowry and then marrying another. I believe this was the specific situation Jesus was referring to in Luke 16:18. Notice the context of this verse.

Luke 16:13-14; 18 **No servant can serve two masters: for either he will hate the one, and love the other; or else he will hold to the one, and despise the other. Ye cannot serve God and mammon. And the Pharisees also, who were cov-**

---

146 Amram, *THE JEWISH LAW OF DIVORCE*, 47-48, 119-121.

etous, heard all these things: and they derided him. 18 Whosoever putteth away his wife, and marrieth another, committeth adultery: and whosoever marrieth her that is put away from her husband committeth adultery.

In this passage we see that the context of Luke chapter 16 is covetousness. In the marriage portion of this chapter, as we have already noticed, we have two present participles in the Greek "put away" and "marry another" followed by the leading verb "committeth adultery." As we have also discovered earlier in this treatise, a present participle is to be seen as occurring simultaneous with the leading verb. From the Greek it appears (to me at least) men were deliberately marrying rich women in order to obtain their wealth to entice or lure an attractive woman in so that they could marry her.[147] Even the most homely man can lure a beautiful woman if he is wealthy. Talk about covetousness, not just money, but money and sexual desire. This type of covetousness seems to be the evil practice Jesus was condemning.

Next we shall take a look at the infamous verse nine and the exception clause to see what conclusions can be drawn.

---

[147] The word "another" in this passage is the Greek word *heteros* which means another of a different kind (our English word heterosexual is derived from this word). This is the same word found in Galatians 1:6 in reference to another (*heteros*) gospel. Luke is indicating a distinction is to be recognized between the first wife and the second wife. That distinction seems to be that of a wealthy first wife in contrast to a sexually appealing second wife. They were marrying one kind of wife to obtain another kind of wife.

CHAPTER VIII: THE EXCEPTION CLAUSE, "PUTTING AWAY" VERSUS "ADULTERY," AND   MARRIAGE ELIGIBILITY

Matthew 19:5-6 **5 and said, For this cause shall a man leave his father and mother, and shall cleave to his wife; and the two shall become one flesh? 6 So that they are no more two, but one flesh. What therefore God hath joined together, let not man put asunder.** (ASV)

1 Timothy 4:1-3 **1 But the Spirit saith expressly, that in later times some shall fall away from the faith, giving heed to seducing spirits and doctrines of demons, 2 through the hypocrisy of men that speak lies, branded in their own conscience as with a hot iron; 3 forbidding to marry.** (ASV)

God is against marriage-breaking and for marriage-making!

Matthew 19:9 **And I say unto you, Whosoever shall put away his wife, <u>except for fornication</u>, and shall marry another, committeth adultery: and he that marrieth her when she is put away committeth adultery.**[148]

What about the "exception clause"? Before we can discuss what the exception clause means, we need to first examine how it is treated by those who hold the traditional view.

General observation indicates that modern culture places a much greater emphasis on the exception clause than scripture. The exception clause is mentioned only two times in scripture, both in Matthew. Neither Mark nor Luke mentions the exception clause. None of the other apostles ever mention the exception clause. Even in Paul's discussion of marriage in 1 Corinthians 7 the exception clause is conspicuously absent. However, in discussions about marriage today the exception clause is <u>the central issue</u>. After divorce all subsequent mar-

---

[148] Underlining added for emphasis.

riages, whether they are approved of or not, hinge on the exception clause.

The traditional view is based on premises already discussed. Namely, the word *apoluo* means "divorce," the word *porneia* means "adultery," and only God joins or disjoins, therefore it is impossible for man to destroy or end a marriage sinfully. The traditional view will then read this passage to say "whosoever shall divorce his wife, except for adultery, and shall marry another, will committeth adultery: and he that marrieth her when she is divorced will committeth adultery." From this is postulated that one who divorces for a cause other than adultery renders the divorce "unscriptural." Therefore, in the eyes of God, the divorce is not recognized, and they are still married to one another. If one or the other marries, God does not recognize the marriage as valid. Therefore, according to the doctrine, the only divorce recognized by God is one in which adultery is the reason for the divorce. As a result, those who have divorced "unscripturally" must remain unmarried, for if they marry another they cannot be forgiven as long as they remain in what is termed an "adulteress marriage." The church then becomes marriage and divorce investigators trying to decide the guilty party or parties. The leaders of the churches must become what amounts to ecclesiastical lawyers trying to unravel all the possible scenarios they may encounter to determine for God if He is going to recognize the divorce or not. So, if the church decides a divorce is valid, then God sees it as valid, and the person may marry another; if the church decides it is not valid, then God does not see it as valid, and they may not marry another. But what if the church gets it wrong?

We have already shown that "put away" does not mean "divorce," "fornication" does not mean "adultery," and "let not put asunder" does not mean "cannot put asunder," and the adultery is committed against the first wife, not with the second wife.

Another problem with the traditional view is reading verse nine (containing the exception clause) out of order in its context. What the traditional view does is take verse nine and makes it Jesus' answer to the first question in verse three, that is, "is it lawful for a man to put away his wife for every cause." By doing so, they take this to mean that verses four through eight are meant to be parenthetical, ignoring the fact (because of preconception) that there were two questions asked by the Pharisees and verse nine follows in sequence the question asked in verse seven.

Matthew 19:3-9 The Pharisees also came unto him, tempting him, and saying unto him, <u>Is it lawful for a man to put away his wife for every cause</u>? And he answered and said unto them, Have ye not read, that he which made them at the beginning made them male and female, And said, For this cause shall a man leave father and mother, and shall cleave to his wife: and they twain shall be one flesh? Wherefore they are no more twain, but one flesh. What therefore God hath joined together, let not man put asunder. They say unto him<u>, Why did Moses then command to give a writing of divorcement, and to put her away</u>? He saith unto them, Moses because of the hardness of your hearts suffered you to put away your wives: but from the beginning it was not so. And I say unto you, Whosoever shall put away his wife, except it be for fornication, and shall marry another, committeth adultery: and whoso marrieth her which is put away doth commit adultery.[149]

The first question and answer is given in verses three through six, notice: **3 The Pharisees also came unto him, tempting him, and saying unto him, Is it lawful for a man to put away his wife for every cause? 4 And he answered and said unto them, Have ye not read, that he which made them at the beginning made them male and female, 5 And said, For this cause shall a man leave father and mother, and shall cleave to his wife: and they twain shall be one flesh? 6 Wherefore they are no more twain, but one flesh. What therefore God hath joined together, let not man put asunder.**

---
[149] Ibid.

Verse nine is not in answer to the question in verse three, but is in answer to the question posed in verse seven, and should look like this: **7 They say unto him, Why did Moses then command to give a writing of divorcement, and to put her away? 8 He saith unto them, Moses because of the hardness of your hearts suffered you to put away your wives: but from the beginning it was not so. 9 And I say unto you, Whosoever shall put away his wife, except it be for fornication, and shall marry another, committeth adultery: and whoso marrieth her which is put away doth commit adultery.** Verse nine is in answer to the Pharisees' perverted interpretation of Deuteronomy 24:1-2, indicated by their question in verse seven. My paraphrase of verses seven through nine: "'Why would Moses command a bill of divorcement if God did not approve of us putting away our wives?' Jesus said, 'Moses did not give the command to give a bill of divorcement because God approved of you putting away your wives, but because you were putting them away, and because of the hardhearted way you were putting them away, without a writing of divorcement. The truth is, God has never (not even from the beginning of time) approved of putting away. And I want you to know not only does God not approve of putting away, but any man who puts away his wife, except in the case of fornication, and marries another to replace her, commits the sin of vow breaking or breaking wedlock against her, and he who marries her when she is put away, not divorced, commits adultery.'"

Verse nine is part of the answer to the second question posed in verse seven. The Pharisees were not asking about marriage eligibility; they were asking about whether it was lawful to put away. Jesus was not saying that a man could marry another in the event his divorcing his wife was because of adultery. He was saying if a man puts away a wife, he commits adultery against her (i.e. breaks wedlock), except in the case of fornication. In the case of fornication he does not commit adultery against his wife (i.e. does not break wedlock). His statement had nothing to do with eligibility to marry another, but with what constitutes adultery against the man's wife.[150] When Jesus said "and I say unto you" He was not contrasting the old law with the new, but He was contrasting the Jews' perversion of Deuteronomy 24 with the truth. That is, "You say God authorized putting away, and I say it is sin. But in the case of fornication, one does not commit adultery or marriage-breaking by putting away, otherwise, he does commit adultery or marriage-breaking by putting away."

Let us look at some bible examples where putting away was not considered adultery or breaking wedlock. Not only were these examples of putting away not adultery, some of them were actually commanded by God.

Prenuptial Sex

Deuteronomy 22:13-21 **If any man take a wife, and go in unto her, and hate her, And give occasions of speech against her, and bring up an evil name upon her, and say, I took this woman, and when I came to her, I found her not a maid: Then shall the father of the damsel, and her mother, take and bring forth the tokens of the damsel's virginity unto the elders of the city in the gate: And the damsel's father shall say unto the elders, I gave my daughter unto this man to wife, and he hateth her; And, lo, he hath given occasions of speech against her, saying, I found not thy daughter a maid; and yet these are the tokens of my daughter's virginity. And they shall spread the cloth before the elders of the city. And the elders of that city shall take that man and chastise him; And they shall amerce him in an hundred shekels of silver, and give them unto the father of the damsel, because he hath brought up an evil name upon a virgin of Israel: and she shall be his wife; he may not put her away all his days. But if this thing be true, and the tokens of virginity be not found for the damsel: Then they shall bring out the damsel to the door of her father's house, and the men of her city shall stone her with stones that she die: because she hath wrought folly in Israel, to play the whore**

---

150 Jesus' concern is the protection of the wife who is totally at the mercy of the husband.

(this is the Hebrew word *zanah* and in the Greek LXX it is from the word *porneia* meaning "fornication") **in her father's house: so shalt thou put evil away from among you.** Notice in the case of a woman marrying a man and afterwards discovering she was not a virgin (i.e. she committed fornication) he may make a public charge against her and put her away and she is to be stoned to death. It is interesting to note that prenuptial sex was not a capital offence in and of itself.

Exodus 22:16-17 And if a man entice a maid that is not betrothed, and lie with her, he shall surely endow her to be his wife. If her father utterly refuse to give her unto him, he shall pay money according to the dowry of virgins.

It seems the reason for the death penalty in the former case is twofold. First is the prenuptial sex (fornication), and second, she falsifies her vows with a pretense of virginity. This second part seems to be the defining factor. Therefore, her vows are false, and the marriage may be terminated without the husband breaking wedlock since the vows were bogus. The man in such cases simply sends the woman home to her father and her father then becomes responsible for her. Notice in verse 21 of Deuteronomy 22 **then they shall bring out the damsel to the <u>door of her father's house</u>, and the men of her city shall stone her to death.**[151] Observe where the men of the city go to get this woman. She is to be found at her father's house. Whether the woman is stoned to death or not is irrelevant to the man, he simply sends the woman back to her father[152] and he does not have to give her a writing of divorcement because the marriage was fallacious. The marriage is invalid because the marriage covenant had not been fulfilled by the other party. The man is no longer responsible for her and is not required to fulfill his duties to her as her husband. Of course, in the case she is put to death, the writing of divorcement would be unnecessary anyway.

---

151 Underlining added for emphasis.
152 The man does not personally stone the woman. Whether she is stoned to death or not does not change his right to put her away. The stoning of the woman becomes the responsibility of the civil authorities.

A similar situation comes to mind; that is the case of Joseph and Mary.

Matthew 1:18-20 **Now the birth of Jesus Christ was on this wise: When as his mother Mary was <u>espoused</u> to Joseph, before they came together, she was found with child of the Holy Ghost. Then Joseph her husband, being a just man, and not willing to make her a publick example, was minded to put her away privily. But while he thought on these things, behold, the angel of the Lord appeared unto him in a dream, saying, Joseph, thou son of David, fear not to take unto thee Mary thy wife: for that which is conceived in her is of the Holy Ghost.**[153] There are several things to notice about this passage. First, the word "husband" is the Greek word *aner* and simply means "man," and could be understood as saying "Joseph her man." Also, the word "wife" is the Greek word *gune* and could be understood as saying "Mary thy woman." Second, the context (verses 18 and 20) indicates that Joseph and Mary were merely engaged or espoused (KJV), not married, at this time. Third, Joseph would not have to give her a writing of divorcement because they were not married. Some modern translations have translated *apoluo* "divorce" instead of "put away," but they have been influenced by the traditional view. The problem comes from a myth that developed over the years (post apostolic) that a betrothal required a divorce. This idea is found in some commentaries, but there is no biblical support for such a notion. This idea is the product of the *Mishna*. In the first century, some Jews (Pharisees in particular) had what was called the "oral law," and basically this oral law was to explain the meaning and application of the written law. Some of these oral laws were those Jesus referred to as "the doctrines of men" (see Matthew 15:9). Sometime after the first century (several hundred years), these laws were written down in what is known as the *Mishna*. What has happened in the case of Joseph and Mary is clarified by Dan Knight in his 2010 article on pages 21-22, quoting Professor Peter Zaas:

> While biblical law makes no provision for divorce

---
153 Underlining added for emphasis.

in the case of a broken betrothal, rabbinic law famously does. The Mishna, for example, so unself-consciously assumes that a betrothal constitutes a marriage, so far as divorce is concerned, that contemporary scholars who get the point at all... generally read the rabbinical situation back into the biblical one, and conclude that biblical law requires a *get*... to dissolve a betrothal as well...

Zaas further comments on the writing of Michael Satlow in this regard:

> Recently Michael Satlow, in his 2001 volume *Jewish Marriage in Antiquity,* notes... Satlow concludes that, while financial damages may be assessed when a betrothed woman is acquired by someone else, the law does not obligate a divorce...[154]

Joseph was going to put Mary away (i.e. send her back to her father), not divorce her. Even if they were married he had the right to send her away without a writ of divorce. Why did he believe he had this right? It seemed evident to him she had committed fornication based upon the fact that she was pregnant.[155]

Illegitimate unions or marriages:

It is also not adultery when one puts away an illegitimate partner; that is, when the marriage is not a lawful marriage. If a marriage was not lawful, then no certificate was needed. There were marriages and relationships in scripture that are described as fornication. In such cases, they were told to put

---

[154] As quoted in Knight, "What Jesus Really Said: Putting Away the Mistranslations about Divorce," 20-21. The following URL was given by Knight for the Zaas article: URL: http://www.biblicallaw.net/2007/zaas.pdf. Unfortunately, this article is no longer accessible at this URL and, although efforts were taken to access the Zaas article, it was unsuccessful. It appears that the article mentioned here is Zaas' article called "Matthew's Birth Story: An Early Milepost in the History of Jewish Marriage Law." Here is the citation for a 2009 version of this article: Zaas, Peter. "Matthew's Birth Story: An Early Milepost in the History of Jewish Marriage Law." *Biblical Theology Bulletin* 39, no. 3 (2009): 125-128. Here is a citation for the Satlow book that Zaas is most likely referencing: Satlow, Michael L. *Jewish Marriage in Antiquity*. Princeton, NJ: Princeton University Press, 2001. Zaas gives a quote from page 69 of the Satlow book, but it is unknown whether the entirety of the information Zaas gathers from the Satlow book is found on page 69. Unfortunately, the exact page number(s) Zaas is referencing is unknown. It is possible that Zaas mentions them in his article, however, access to this article was not obtained.

[155] Knight, "What Jesus Really Said: Putting Away the Mistranslations about Divorce," 19.

away their unlawful partner, and no writ of divorce was required because the marriage was not legitimate from the start. Let's look at a few.

Matthew 14:3-4 For Herod had laid hold on John, and bound him, and put him in prison for Herodias' sake, his brother Philip's wife. For John said unto him, It is not lawful for thee to have her. (KJV) **Matthew 14:3-4 3 For Herod had laid hold on John, and bound him, and put him in prison for the sake of Herodias, his brother Philip's wife. 4 For John said unto him, It is not lawful for thee to have her.** (ASV) Some claim this proves the traditional view in that John was condemning Herod for marrying an "unscripturally divorced" woman. Let us examine a few facts and see if the facts support this contention. First: divorce is not mentioned anywhere in these passages. In fact, God does not say Herodias divorced Phillip, rather the passage says Herodias was at that time Philip's wife (v. 3). Divorce is not the issue here, because there was no divorce even mentioned. Some claim history records Herodias divorced Philip. We must be cognizant of the fact historians do not function as exegetes, but are recorders of how events are perceived in a point and time in history. Of course, history as seen by people in any point in time will not change the word of God, especially those outside God's covenant. The word of God always trumps commentators and historians, and the views of society. Josephus did say Herodias divorced Phillip,[156] and since Jewish women could not give a writing of divorcement to a man, she would had to have divorced him "Roman style," that is, she simply left him; she did not divorce him. It is possible Josephus is not using the word "divorce" in the sense of an official or formal divorce, but he could be using the word in the sense of simply separating her-

---

156 Josephus, *THE ANTIQUITIES OF THE JEWS*, contained within Whiston's *THE WORKS OF JOSEPHUS: Complete and Unabridged*, 485. Josephus says in *ANTIQUITIES OF THE JEWS*, Book 18, Chapter 5: "…but Herodias, their sister, was married to Herod [Phillip], the son of Herod the great, who was born of Mariamne, the daughter of Simon the high priest, who had daughter, Salome; after whose birth Herodias took upon her to confound the laws of our country, and divorce herself from her husband while he was alive, and was married to Herod [Antipas], her husband's brother by the father's side…" (underlining added for emphasis).

self from Phillip. Regardless, Matthew by inspiration does not mention divorce and he says she was, at the time, married to Phillip, not divorced. Second: John did not say Herod could not have Herodias because she was divorced and her divorce was not scriptural. Herod, Herodias, and Phillip, as well as John, were living under the Law of Moses at the time. In fact, John died under the law. Under the law a woman who was divorced could marry another lawfully (Deuteronomy 24:1-2). If Herodias was divorced, she could marry another man lawfully, but she could not marry her husband's brother lawfully. It is inconceivable that John was binding New Testament law on Herod who was not subject to the New Testament at this point in time. Herod did not put John in prison because he taught contrary to the New Testament law, but because John rightly accused Herod of acts against the Old Testament law. Leviticus 18:16 **Thou shalt not uncover the nakedness of thy brother's wife: it is thy brother's nakedness.** Leviticus 20:21 **And if a man shall take his brother's wife, it is an unclean thing: he hath uncovered his brother's nakedness; they shall be childless.** John was not rebuking Herod on the basis of the traditional view of marriage, divorce, and remarriage. Instead, his rebuke was according to the law of incest recorded in Leviticus. Under the Law of Moses, having one's brother's wife while the brother was still living was forbidden. In this case Herod would not have been breaking wedlock since the marriage was illicit. He was required under the Law to end the relationship and send Herodias back to her husband. Here, putting away was not adultery; in fact, it was required by God to be done.

Another is: 1 Corinthians 5:1 **It is reported commonly that there is fornication among you, and such fornication as is not so much as named among the Gentiles, that one should have his father's wife.** Again, the traditionalist claims this is an example of divorce and remarriage being forbidden. But, notice Paul said this type of fornication is not even accepted among the Gentiles. Surely this could not be divorce and remarriage since divorce and remarriage was commonly practiced among the gentiles of the first century without any stigma whatsoever. Divorce and remarriage was almost as common as sandals among the Gentiles in those days. It is not at all beyond reason to conclude this man was living with his step-mom based on the gravity of the sin expressed by Paul (something even the gentiles would have opposed). It is very possible the woman was not divorced from the boy's father. It is stated in the passage she is his father's wife, not she was his father's wife. In this case, certainly ending this relationship was warranted. The son needed to end the relationship and send his father's wife away. Not only is putting away not adultery in this case, it is demanded by God.

Another is referred to in Jude 1:7: **Even as Sodom and Gomorrha, and the cities about them in like manner, giving themselves over to fornication, and going after strange flesh, are set forth for an example, suffering the vengeance of eternal fire.** We know from Genesis 19:4-8 the practice of fornication among Sodom and Gomorrah was homosexuality. The union between people of the same sex is fornication, and putting away a same sex partner is certainly not adultery. The relationship must end, and it may be necessary to satisfy the requirements of civil law with a certificate of divorce. Regardless, whether a certificate of divorce is required or not, the certificate of divorce is irrelevant. To end the relationship would not be adultery, as a matter of fact, it is commanded by God that it end. Some may say "here is a case where God is forbidding someone from marrying." To say Brother So-N-So cannot marry Brother What's-His-Name is not the same as saying Brother So-N-So cannot marry anyone, or is forbidden to marry altogether. It is one thing to say a person cannot marry some people and another thing to say they are forbidden to marry anyone. Ephesians 5:3 **But fornication, and all uncleanness, or covetousness, let it not be once named among you, as becometh saints;**

Even if Jesus had not mentioned the exception clause, common sense would tell us it would not be a sin to break an unlawful union; it would go without saying. In fact, Jesus did not mention the exception clause in Mark and Luke's account. It would not be a sin to break a homosexual union; as a matter of fact, it would be a sin not to break such a union.

UNFAITHFULNESS:

Isaiah 50:1 **Thus saith the LORD, Where is the bill of your mother's divorcement, whom I have put away? or which of my creditors is it to whom I have sold you? Behold, for your iniquities have ye sold yourselves, and for your transgressions is your mother put away.** Here God said He "put away" Judah because of her unfaithfulness.

2 Chronicles 21:11 **11 Moreover he made high places in the mountains of Judah, and made the inhabitants of Jerusalem to play the harlot, and led Judah astray.** (ASV)

2 Chronicles 21:11 **11 Moreover he made high places in the mountains of Judah, and caused the inhabitants of Jerusalem to commit fornication, and compelled Judah thereto.** (KJV)

There is no indication that God ever divorced Judah, but He did put her away. He put her away to encourage her to repent (see Isaiah 54: 5-10). His intent in putting her away was for the purpose of salvaging the marriage, not to repudiate her as was the case with the Pharisees whom Jesus rebuked.[157] It was not adultery for God to put away Judah because she had already broken her vows (i.e. committed adultery) through her fornication; she was unfaithful to her marriage vows. Many couples today have had their marriages restored after one has committed fornication because the innocent spouse put away the other to bring them to repentance, which resulted in forgiveness and reconciliation. This is a biblical approach to a case where one's spouse has been unfaithful. If the spouse refuses to repent, it may become necessary to end the marriage through divorce as God did with Israel (Jeremiah 3:8, cf. 2 Kings 17:18).

---

157 This biblical principle is equivalent to that of the church expressed in 1 Corinthians 5.

One would not commit adultery by putting away an unfaithful spouse because adultery would have already been committed through the act or acts of fornication of his or her spouse.

Finally, we have a discourse between Jesus and His disciples concerning these things.

Matthew 19:10-12 **His disciples say unto him, If the case of the man be so with his wife, it is not good to marry. But he said unto them, All men cannot receive this saying, save they to whom it is given. For there are some eunuchs, which were so born from their mother's womb: and there are some eunuchs, which were made eunuchs of men: and there be eunuchs, which have made themselves eunuchs for the kingdom of heaven's sake. He that is able to receive it, let him receive it.** This is what I think was being said by the disciples of Jesus and His response. His disciples, after hearing Jesus, decided it might be better not to marry at all; but why? Because Jesus had just revoked their wife-swapping privileges. They were under the understanding that if for some reason they decided they no longer wanted their wife around they could just replace her, but Jesus basically says, *"No, if you take a wife you are responsible for her for life."* In that case (they were thinking) if you marry a women and she turns out to be a nag or unpleasant to live with or you come to hate her, you are stuck with her because to put her away would be adultery, so they reasoned, *"Maybe it would be better not to marry at all."* Jesus says in response, *"Not everyone is capable to live without marriage. There are those who can, namely those who were born eunuchs, those who have been made eunuchs by others, and those who have made themselves eunuchs* (i.e. those who can contain: 1 Corinthians 7:9) *for the kingdom's sake. Therefore, those who are capable of celibacy, if they prefer to not marry, then fine, they do not have to marry if that is their preference."* However, Jesus points out that not all are able to receive this saying.[158]

---

[158] In this paragraph, the conversation in italics is a rendering of the conversation between Jesus and the Pharisees, and then His disciples, as found in Matthew 19:8-12, which has been paraphrased, along with supplied information which may help to clarify Jesus' points.

If a marriage has been destroyed, the humane and right thing to do is officially end the marriage with a writing of divorcement so that recovery can take place. This is evident from Mark 10:1-12 **And he arose from thence, and cometh into the coasts of Judaea by the farther side of Jordan: and the people resort unto him again; and, as he was wont, he taught them again. And the Pharisees came to him, and asked him, Is it lawful for a man to put away his wife? tempting him. And he answered and said unto them, What did Moses command you? And they said, Moses suffered to write a bill of divorcement, and to put her away. And Jesus answered and said unto them, For the hardness of your heart he wrote you this precept. But from the beginning of the creation God made them male and female. For this cause shall a man leave his father and mother, and cleave to his wife; And they twain shall be one flesh: so then they are no more twain, but one flesh. What therefore God hath joined together, let not man put asunder. And in the house his disciples asked him again of the same matter. And he saith unto them, Whosoever shall put away his wife, and marry another, committeth adultery against her. And if a woman shall put away her husband, and be married to another, she committeth adultery.** When the Pharisees asked Jesus if it was lawful for a man to put away his wife, Jesus responded with the question: **"What did Moses command you?"** This question was given to convict these Jews who were putting away their wives without a writing of divorcement as God had commanded them to do. They replied: **"Moses suffered to write a bill of divorcement, and to put her away"** meaning Moses said "you have the option of putting away your wife with the writing of divorcement" implying that one also had the option to put away without the writing of divorcement. Jesus essentially responds by saying "to the contrary, Moses said if you are going to send away a wife, do not leave her in a state of despair and destitution, but you are commanded to give her a writing of divorcement so that she can have a means to lawfully marry another for her wellbeing and recovery." Jesus then goes on to point out that just because Moses commanded the writing of divorcement be given it did not excuse them of the sin of breaking the one flesh relationship, and by doing so they were committing the sin of breaking wedlock against their wives. He went on to say if a woman leaves her husband, then she too is guilty of breaking wedlock.

CONCLUSION:

Before moving from the statements of Jesus to the teaching of Paul on this subject, let me explain my approach to the statements of Jesus, in particular, Matthew 19:9. I tried to define words according to how they are used in scripture rather than relying primarily on dictionaries or lexicons. I have tried to present the plain statements of scripture; that is, just looking at the passages as they are expressly stated. Your attention has been called to the fact that the discussion between the Pharisees and Jesus was not about whether the divorced may marry, but about whether the married may break marriage. When the passages are approached from the perspective of marriage eligibility, the scope and import of the passages are completely changed. Your attention has been called to the fact that the statements made by Jesus should be taken just as they are stated rather than from the perspective of how God sees the situation as opposed to how it is seen by man. My question to this approach is *How do we know how God sees things apart from what is revealed in scripture? In other words, How can we know the mind of God or how God views any matter unless the word of God tells us that is how God sees it?* We need to be very careful when we presume to speak for God and how He sees things. Unless the scripture tells us that "this is what God thinks about this matter or any other," we should let the scripture speak for itself and accept what is written.

The traditional view punishes innocent people. Consider these three scenarios. First: A man murders his wife. Later, he repents and is cleansed by the blood of Jesus and marries again. Most, if not all, would say his second marriage is scriptural and approved of by God. Second: A man, not having ever been married, lives a life of a fornicator and philanderer. He repents and is cleansed by the blood of Jesus. He then meets a woman and marries her. Most, if not all, would say his marriage is scriptural and approved of by God. Third: A man marries his only love and remains faithful to her, but she divorces him. This man may not ever marry again. He must remain celibate. The only man of the three who did the right thing all along in regards to his faithfulness to his wife and lived the way God would have one to live in regards to this matter is the only one who is not free to marry. This man is the only one of the three in which God would deem (according to the traditional view) "it is good that man should be alone"![159]

Proverbs 17:15 **He that justifieth the wicked, and he that condemneth the just, even they both are abomination to the LORD.**

Proverbs 17:26 **Also to punish the just is not good, nor to strike princes for equity.**

Proverbs 18:5 **It is not good to accept the person of the wicked, to overthrow the righteous in judgment.**

When presented with this problem, two objections have been offered in response. First: what about the man or woman who cannot find someone to marry? Second: what about one who has a wife or husband injured and made an invalid? It is true life is not fair and bad things happen to good people because time and chance happens to us all. But it is clear from passages such as Genesis 2:18, 1 Corinthians 7:2, 1 Corinthians 7:8-9, 1 Corinthians 7:28, and Hebrews 13:4 that God approves of marriage for all people and forbids marriage to no one today. Forbidding marriage is a doctrine of demons, not God. Can anyone show where God forbids marriage to anyone today? It will not do to show where God has forbidden some people from marrying certain people, which is not the same as forbidding those same people from marrying anyone. It will not

---

[159] The example of the three men scenario is taken from the Olan Hicks - Mac Deaver debate on Divorce and remarriage. Olan Hicks and Mac Deaver, *Olan Hicks - Mac Deaver Debate On Marriage and Remarriage*, (Searcy, AR: Gospel Enterprises; Austin, TX: Biblical Notes, 1995), 93, 94.

do to say Matthew 5:32, Matthew 19:9, Mark 10:11, and Luke 16:18 forbid marriage, because they simply do not. What they forbid is marriage-breaking, not marriage-making, and appealing to these passages as instances of God forbidding marriage is a clear case of begging the question. Although some may not be married who want to be married, God does not forbid them to marry.

CHAPTER IX: 1 CORINTHIANS 7 AND PAUL

Matthew 19:5-6 **And said, For this cause shall a man leave father and mother, and shall cleave to his wife: and they twain shall be one flesh? Wherefore they are no more twain, but one flesh. What therefore God hath joined together, let not man put asunder.**

1 Timothy 4:1-3 **Now the Spirit speaketh expressly, that in the latter times some shall depart from the faith, giving heed to seducing spirits, and doctrines of devils; Speaking lies in hypocrisy; having their conscience seared with a hot iron; Forbidding to marry, and commanding to abstain from meats, which God hath created to be received with thanksgiving of them which believe and know the truth.**
God is against marriage-breaking and for marriage-making!

1 Corinthians 7:1 **Now concerning the things whereof ye wrote unto me: It is good for a man not to touch a woman.**

Alexander Campbell, in his translation THE LIVING ORACLES NEW TESTAMENT, translates this passage thus: 1 Corinthians 7:1: **Now, concerning the things of which you wrote me: It is good for a man not to marry a woman.** (Oracl)

Without going into too much detail, let me just say that Paul in this portion of his letter (the seventh chapter) is without a doubt favoring celibacy. You cannot read this chapter and come away with any other conclusion. Paul gives two reasons for his preference to celibacy. First: he gives as a reason "the present distress" (verse 26). The nature of the "present distress" is not stated, but was certainly known by the Corinthians. Some think it may have been the persecution under Nero by the Romans. Second: he gives as a reason the fact that a family could be a hindrance to evangelism (verses 32-35). A man might not hesitate to preach Christ even under threat of death, but he might not be as willing if his family were in danger. Under the existing political climate it may have been much more difficult for a professing Christian to provide for one's family. The word "good" in this passage is the Greek *kalos* and is sometimes translated "better" or "well," meaning it was advantageous under the circumstances to be celibate. Not that celibate people are more holy than those who are married but they are less distracted, and loyalties are not as divided. However, Paul is not promoting some ascetic bent, he makes it clear marriage itself is not a sin, nor is it a hindrance to one's personal relationship to God, and in some cases, it is a necessity to moral purity. Paul discourages the dissolution of existing marriages and encourages those who desire to marry to do so without guilt.

We will not examine the entire chapter, but will deal with the verses most commonly referenced in regards to MDR. Before going into specifics on these passages, let me begin with a quote from William Barclay:

> The student of the bible must study the Bible honestly. This is to say, he must go to the Bible to find and to seek truth, and not to prove a case about which he has already made up his mind. It is common – it is almost usual – for people to use the Bible as an arsenal of proof texts to prove things about which they have already made up their minds. A man can use the Bible to find in it what he wants to find. He can use it to hear the echo of his own voice rather than the sound voice of God. Tyndale once said that the students who were taught by the priests and the monks came to the Bible "armed with false principles, with which they are clean shut out of the understanding of scripture."[160]

---

160 William Barclay, Introducing the Bible, (Nashville: Abingdon Press, 1972), 93. Tyndale's quote is from his work The Practice of Prelates…, originally published in Marburg, Germany with Hans Luft's press in 1530. It was reprinted in Tyndale, William. "The Practice of Prelates," a book in a collection of books by Tyndale and John Firth called The Works of the English Reformers: William Tyndale and John Frith, Volume 1, Thomas Russell, editor. London: Ebenezer Palmer, 1831. Digitized and made available

The statements of Paul in 1 Corinthians 7 are not difficult passages; the language is not poetic or allegoric, but rather his statements are straightforward and explicit. If we just take Paul's statements as they are stated, there would not be any controversy concerning them. The problem comes from the fact Paul's statements taken as they are stated conflicts with the traditional view. Those who hold the traditional view try to harmonize their interpretation of Jesus' statements on marriage with those of Paul. They reverse the order of proper hermeneutics by having Jesus interpreting what Paul said instead of Paul interpreting what Jesus said. Having Jesus explain what Paul meant is to reverse the order of correct bible interpretation. The apostles were to be the revealers of all that Jesus said, not the other way around. John 14:26 **But the Comforter, which is the Holy Ghost, whom the Father will send in my name, he shall teach you all things, and bring all things to your remembrance, whatsoever I have said unto you.**

Another important aspect of Paul's statements is the conspicuous absence of the exception clause. If the exception clause was of the importance given to it by the traditional view, certainly Paul would have expressed it on at least a few occasions during this discourse. Those who hold the traditional view will, in their commentaries, import the exception clause into several of Paul's statements. Why the absence? Because Paul was not dealing with unlawful marriages or unions, those classified as fornication such as incest, cohabitation, or homosexual. Paul is dealing with legitimate marriages in this chapter; therefore, the exception clause would have no bearing on these relationships under Paul's purview. Paul discusses or infers remarriage on at least a couple of occasions in this chapter, but never mentions fornication as a factor or qualification required for such marriages. This is <u>one of the reasons I understand Jesus to be speaking of mar-</u>
by Harvard University and accessed on Google Books. URL: https://books.google.com/books?id=o1ssQGn1UvEC&pg=PP12&source=gbs_selected_pages&cad=2#v=onepage&q&f=false (accessed 6/28/17), page in digitized reprint 437.

riage-breaking, not marriage eligibility. If Jesus was speaking of marriage eligibility, then Paul would not have let such an important fact go unnoticed!

1 Corinthians 7:2-9 **Nevertheless, because of sexual immorality, let each man have his own wife, and let each woman have her own husband. Let the husband render to his wife the affection due her, and likewise also the wife to her husband. The wife does not have authority over her own body, but the husband does. And likewise the husband does not have authority over his own body, but the wife does. Do not deprive one another except with consent for a time, that you may give yourselves to fasting and prayer; and come together again so that Satan does not tempt you because of your lack of self-control. But I say this as a concession, not as a commandment. For I wish that all men were even as I myself. But each one has his own gift from God, one in this manner and another in that. But I say to the unmarried and to the widows: It is good for them if they remain even as I am; but if they cannot exercise self-control, let them marry. For it is better to marry than to burn with passion.** (NKJV) I will not say much concerning these verses since we have already covered them in earlier chapters. I do want to say here that God has given marriage as a means of avoiding fornication. This is another reason for rejecting the traditional view. The traditional view would have it that all those who have sinned against marriage must find another way to avoid fornication and deal with that which is described as "burning with passion." When Jesus' disciples said that it might be better not to marry in Matthew 19:10, Jesus responded by saying: **"...all men cannot receive this saying..."**[161] The word "cannot" in this passage is the Greek word *"ou"* meaning an absolute or definite "not." There is a word for "not" in Greek that is iffy, it is the Greek word *"me"* and means "may not" or "should not." When I have pointed this out, some have presented me with some "what if" scenarios, as if God's word could be set aside in this manner. We do not set aside what the bible says

---
161 Matthew 19:11b.

about Baptism because of those "what if" scenarios we often encounter. There are those who have suggested ways other than marriage for avoiding fornication, some reasonable and some not so much. I am not opposed to good advice except when one elevates it to a status equal to a command of God.

Jim McGuiggan said in his commentary on 1 Corinthians:

> The trouble with so many leaders today is that they can't tell the difference between their good advice and the commands of God. They throw around good advice and if the people they're advising don't take that advice, they are offended. Good advice about how often we ought to pray, how often we ought to meet to study the scriptures, how much money we ought to contribute, how we ought to go about doing our evangelism, and the like. It doesn't take long for good advice to rise to the level of God's commands. And those who don't happen to share our views on what ought to be done and how often it should be done, are viewed as rebelling against God's commands.[162]

1 Corinthians 7:8-9 8 But I say to the unmarried and to the widows: It is good for them if they remain even as I am; 9 but if they cannot exercise self-control, let them marry. For it is better to marry than to burn with passion. (NKJV)

Paul is speaking to the unmarried and says it is better for them to stay or remain as he is i.e. unmarried, but he says this "by permission," or in his opinion (according to verse six), and he gives the reason in verse 26- because of the present distress. Did Paul mean it was better for them to remain unmarried for the rest of their lives? Likely he meant for as long as the present distress lasts. The word "remain" is an interesting word, and when we get to verse 11, we will have something to say about the word and its uses in scripture. The word "unmarried" is the Greek word *"agamos,"* the negative form of *gamos*. The word *"gamos"* can refer to the state of being married; for ex-

---
[162] Jim McGuiggan, *THE BOOK OF 1 CORINTHIANS*, (*Looking Into The Bible Series)*, (Lubbock, TX: Montex Publishing Company, 1984), 112.

ample, in verse ten Paul says "now to the married *(gamos)* I command." Or it can (and most often does) refer to the <u>act of getting married</u>; for example, in verse nine Paul says "but if they cannot exercise self-control, let them marry *(gamos).*" Verse ten refers to the state of marriage while verse nine refers to entering into a marriage or the act of getting married. The negative form *"agamos,"* therefore, can mean either "the unmarried state" or "the act of not entering into a marriage with someone." This is an important distinction as we shall see when we get to verses 10 and 11. Paul here is referring to the unmarried state. The "unmarried" in this context refers to those who have been divorced, never married, and/or widowed (both men and women). Notice he does not say those "divorced scripturally," he simply says "unmarried," that is, those who are in a state of being unmarried, including all those who have divorced, regardless of the reason.

Are those who are divorced unmarried in the same sense as the virgin and widow? Notice the conversation of Jesus and the woman of Samaria. John 4:16-18 **Jesus saith unto her, Go, call thy husband, and come hither. The woman answered and said, I have no husband. Jesus said unto her, Thou hast well said, I have no husband: For thou hast had five husbands; and he whom thou now hast is not thy husband: in that saidst thou truly.** This passage indicates Jesus regarded divorce as an end to one's marriage (unless one takes the highly unlikely position this woman had been widowed five times and still be young enough to attract a live-in man). It would not be unreasonable to conclude that she had been divorced at least a few times, if not five times. Since Jesus said she had no husband and if only one marriage ended in divorce, we must conclude divorce ends the marriage. In every case where the writing of divorcement was given in scripture the marriage was terminated. When God gave Israel the writing of divorcement, she and God were no longer married! Jeremiah 3:8 **And I saw, when for all the causes whereby backsliding Israel committed adultery I had put her away, and given her a bill of divorce; yet her treacherous sister Judah feared not,**

but went and played the harlot also. 2 Kings 17:6 **In the ninth year of Hoshea the king of Assyria took Samaria, and carried Israel away into Assyria, and placed them in Halah and in Habor by the river of Gozan, and in the cities of the Medes.** 2 Kings 17:18 **Therefore the LORD was very angry with Israel, and removed them out of his sight: there was none left but the tribe of Judah only.** When God commanded the writing of divorcement be given (Deuteronomy 24:1-2), it was given to end the marriage.

1 Corinthians 7:10-11 **10 Now to the married I command, yet not I but the Lord: A wife is not to depart from her husband. 11 But even if she does depart, let her remain unmarried or be reconciled to her husband. And a husband is not to divorce his wife.** (NKJV) These verses are important verses because they are often used to support the traditional view. Some major assumptions are made about these passages that are not consistent with the text. Allow me to give you the traditional view and then we shall examine the text and see if it supports the traditional view. According to the traditional view, this passage is referring to a woman who has divorced her husband, and Paul is saying she must either remain celibate the rest of her life, or remarry her ex-husband. There are some problems with this view, so let us examine them.

Notice Paul is speaking to the married, not the unmarried; he spoke to the unmarried in verses eight and nine. He is not talking about those who have divorced, but to those who are married. Paul, in verse ten, says those who are married should not break their covenant or marriage vows; to be precise, it is what Paul said Jesus said. Jesus said do not "put asunder" your marriage i.e. do not break your "one flesh" relationship (Mathew 19:6). Paul was not referring to what Jesus said in Matthew 19:9 or Matthew 19:12, as some have suggested, but to what He said in verse 6 of Matthew 19. The Greek word translated "put asunder" in Matthew 19:6 is the exact same word translated "depart" in 1 Corinthians 7:10. Paul, by using the same word as Jesus, is making a direct link to verse six of

Matthew 19. The word "depart" is the Greek word *chorizo* and does not mean "divorce." This is a very important distinction, and I will now attempt to prove this point.

First: Let us examine what the experts say. I have not found any scholars who define *chorizo* as "divorce," that is, in the technical sense. Some of the better lexicons will give the definition of the word in italics which is the technical definition of the word. In lexicons, the words in italics are the definition of the words; the non-italicized words are the commentary of the lexicographer i.e. how he thinks the word is being used in a particular verse. Taking into consideration that most all lexicographers accept the traditional view of marriage, with its roots in the Catholic Church, it should not be surprising to find them saying "as to divorce" in regards to some marriage passages. However, some make no mention of divorce in reference to the meaning of *chorizo,* even though they view marriage from the traditional perspective. For example, W.E. Vine does not put *Chorizo* under "divorce," but under "separate."[163] Strong's does not mention divorce as a definition.[164] William D. Mounce, in his *Analytical Lexicon To The Greek New Testament* does not give "divorce" as a definition of *chorizo.*[165] Thayer, as well as Bauer, Arndt, Gingrich (BAG) do not give "divorce" as a definition (i.e. words in italics) but say "of divorce" in their commentary portion.[166] We must keep in mind the comments not in italics are in the view of the lexicographer.[167] Even in the case of Thayer, if you read further in his lexicon it appears he is using the word "divorce" in the sense of breaking the relationship, not in the sense of dissolving the marriage officially. The same may be said of A.T. Robertson in his commentary *New Testament Word Pictures.*[168]

---

163 Vine, W. E., *An Expository Dictionary of New Testament Words: With their Precise Meanings for English Readers, Volume III,* (Old Tappan, NJ: Fleming H. Revell Company, 1966), 346.
164 Strong's #5563. "From 5561; to place room between, i.e. part; reflexively, to go away:--depart, put asunder, separate. See Greek 5561 (chora)." From: Strong, James, STRONG'S EXHAUSTIVE CONCORDANCE OF THE BIBLE, *Dictionary of the Hebrew Bible, Dictionary of the Greek Testament,* 78.
165 William D. Mounce, *THE ANALYTICAL LEXICON TO THE GREEK NEW TESTAMENT,* (Grand Rapids, MI: Zondervan, 1993), 485.
166 Joseph H. Thayer, *THAYER'S GREEK-ENGLISH LEXICON OF THE NEW TESTAMENT: Coded to Strong's Numbering System,* (2009), 674. Walter Bauer, William F. Arndt, and F. Wilbur Gingrich, *A GREEK ENGLISH LEXICON OF THE NEW TESTAMENT,* 898.
167 See Thayer's comments in chapter III concerning the lexicographer's acknowledged significations of a word.
168 Archibald Thomas Robertson, *Word Pictures in the New Testament,* commentary for 1 Corinthians 7:10.

Second: I examined several translations to see how the Greek scholars translated the word *"chorizo"* in their translations and this is what I found.[169]

1 Corinthians 7:10-11 **10 And unto the married I command, yet not I, but the Lord, Let not the wife <u>depart</u> from her husband: 11 But and if she <u>depart,</u> let her remain unmarried, or be reconciled to her husband: and let not the husband put away his wife.** (KJV)

1 Corinthians 7:10-11 **10 But unto the married I give charge, yea not I, but the Lord, That the wife <u>depart</u> not from her husband 11 (but should she <u>depart</u>, let her remain unmarried, or else be reconciled to her husband); and that the husband leave not his wife.** (ASV)

1 Corinthians 7:10-11 **10 But to the married I give orders, though not I but the Lord, that the wife may not <u>go away</u> from her husband 11 (Or if she <u>goes away</u> from him, let her keep unmarried, or be united to her husband again); and that the husband may not go away from his wife.** (BBE)

1 Corinthians 7:10-11 **10 But to the married I enjoin, not *I*, but the Lord, Let not wife be <u>separated</u> from husband; 11 (but if also she shall have <u>been separated</u>, let her remain unmarried, or be reconciled to her husband;) and let not husband leave wife.** (DBY)

1 Corinthians 7:10-11 **10 Now to the married *Christians* I give instruction (not I but the Lord),** *the wife* **is not to <u>leave</u> her husband. 11. But if she does <u>leave</u>** *him,* **she is to remain unmarried, or be reconciled to the husband: and** *the* **husband is not to leave** *his* **wife.** (ESB)[170]

1 Corinthians 7:10-11 **10 To the married I give this charge (not I, but the Lord): the wife should not <u>separate</u> from her husband 11 (but if she does, she should remain unmarried <u>or else be</u> reconciled to her husband), and the husband**

---
169 Underlining has been added to the following passages in this section.
170 Harold Littrell, translator, *The English Study Bible: New Testament*, (Ft. Worth, TX: Star Bible Publications, 1994), 271.

should not divorce his wife. (ESV)

1 Corinthians 7:10-11 **10 But to those already married my commandment is--and not mine, but the Lord's--that a wife is not to <u>leave</u> her husband; 11 (or if she has already <u>left</u> him let her either remain as she is, or be reconciled to him), and also that a husband is not to put away his wife.** (MNT)

1 Corinthians 7:10-11 **But to the married I give instructions, not I, but the Lord, that the wife should not <u>leave</u> her husband 11 (but if she does <u>leave</u>, she must remain unmarried, or else be reconciled to her husband), and that the husband should not divorce his wife.** (NASB)

1 Corinthians 7:10-11 **10 Now to the married I command, yet not I but the Lord: A wife is not to <u>depart</u> from her husband. 11 But even if she does <u>depart</u>, let her remain unmarried or be reconciled to her husband. And a husband is not to divorce his wife.** (NKJV)

1 Corinthians 7:10-11 **10 Now, those who have married I charge, (yet not I, but the Lord;) let not a wife <u>depart</u> from her husband: 11 but if she even <u>depart</u>, let her remain unmarried, or be reconciled to her husband; and a husband must not put away his wife.** (Oracl)

1 Corinthians 7:10-11 **10 To the married I give charge (not I but the Lord), that the wife not <u>separate</u> from her husband. 11 But if she does <u>separate</u>, let her remain unmarried, or be reconciled to her husband, and that the husband not leave his wife.** (TEG)

1 Corinthians 7:10-11 **10 To those who are married my direction is-yet it is not mine, but the Master's-that a woman is not to <u>leave</u> her husband 11 (If she has done so, let her remain as she is, or else be reconciled to her husband) and also that a man is not to divorce his wife.** (TCNT)

1 Corinthians 7:10-11 **10 But to the married I command--**

not I, but the Lord--that the wife not <u>leave</u> her husband 11 (but if she <u>departs</u>, let her remain unmarried, or else be reconciled to her husband), and that the husband not leave his wife. (WEB)

1 Corinthians 7:10-11 **10 But to those already married my instructions are--yet not mine, but the Lord's--that a wife is not to <u>leave</u> her husband; 11 or if she has already <u>left</u> him, let her either remain as she is or be reconciled to him; and that a husband is not to send away his wife.** (WNT)

1 Corinthians 7:10-11 **10 and to the married I announce--not I, but the Lord--let not a wife separate from a husband: 11 but and if she may <u>separate</u>, let her remain unmarried, or to the husband let her be reconciled, and let not a husband send away a wife.** (YLT)

1 Corinthians 7:10-11 **10 Vnto the maryed comaunde not I but the Lorde: that the wyfe <u>separate</u> not her selfe from the man. 11 Yf she <u>separate</u> her selfe let her remayne vnmaryed or be reconciled vnto her husbande agayne. And let not the husbande put awaye his wyfe from him.** (TYNDALE'S [1535])

1 Corinthians 7:10-11 **10 But to hem that ben ioyned in matrymonye, Y comaunde, not Y, but the Lord, that the wijf <u>departe</u> not fro the hosebonde; 11 and that if sche <u>departith</u>, that sche dwelle vnweddid, or be recounselid to hir hosebonde; and the hosebonde forsake not the wijf.** (WYCLIFF'S [1385])

I also checked the following translations: AMP, KJVA, BOOKS, CEB, CEVDCUS06, CPDV, DRC, ERV (easy to read version), GNB, GNBDK, GNT, GW, GWC, HCSB, ISR98, LEB, MKJV, MSG, NABRE, NCV, NIRV, NIV, NLT, NRSV, OJB, RSV, RV1885, SEB, TLV,

None of these translations translated *chorizo* "divorce." I could have listed more, but I got tired of writing, and these are sufficient to make my point. The Greek scholars who worked on these translations, supply enough evidence to confirm the word *chorizo* does not mean divorce.

Third: how does the word of God define *chorizo?* Look how the word *chorizo* is used in verses other than those pertaining to marriage in the NT. The following passages are all other passages in the New Testament containing the word *chorizo*.[171]

Acts 1:4 **And, being assembled together with them, commanded them that they should not <u>depart</u> from Jerusalem, but wait for the promise of the Father, which, saith he, ye have heard of me.**

Acts 18:1-2 **After these things Paul departed from Athens, and came to Corinth; And found a certain Jew named Aquila, born in Pontus, lately come from Italy, with his wife Priscilla; (because that Claudius had commanded all Jews to <u>depart</u> from Rome:) and came unto them.**

Romans 8:35 **Who shall <u>separate</u> us from the love of Christ? shall tribulation, or distress, or persecution, or famine, or nakedness, or peril, or sword?**

Romans 8:39 **Nor height, nor depth, nor any other creature, shall be able to <u>separate</u> us from the love of God, which is in Christ Jesus our Lord.**

Philemon 1:15 **For perhaps he therefore <u>departed</u> for a season, that thou shouldest receive him for ever;**

Hebrews 7:26 **For such an high priest became us, who is holy, harmless, undefiled, <u>separate</u> from sinners, and made higher than the heavens;**

It should be obvious divorce is not inherent in the meaning of *chorizo.* The word *chorizo* is not used for "divorce" in any of these passages. The word *chorizo* may be used in a passage that has divorce as its subject, but one cannot tell if divorce is

---
171 Underlining has been added to the following passages in this section.

the subject of the passage by the use of the word *chorizo* since divorce is not the meaning of the word. The only way to tell if the passage is discussing divorce is by an exegesis of the passage or if there is another word in the passage which inherently means divorce (i.e. *apostasion,* Strong's #647). Those who come to this passage saying *chorizo* is referring to divorce are assuming that which they intend to prove. The word in the context of 1 Corinthians 7 that refers to divorce is found in verses 27-28 **27 Art thou bound unto a wife? seek not to be loosed. Art thou loosed** *(lelusai)* **from a wife? seek not a wife. 28 But and if thou marry, thou hast not sinned;**[172] Notice Paul did not use *chorizo* when he was clearly referring to divorce.

What about the word "unmarried" in verse 11? Those who hold the traditional view will point to this word as proof these passages are talking of divorce. So let us examine this proposition to see if they have a case. Those who take this view will meet themselves coming. Those who take the traditional view, if they claim an "unscripturally divorced" person is unmarried in the same sense as the "unmarried" in verses eight and nine, must abandon the view that an "unscripturally divorced" person is not unmarried; that is, they cannot claim the "unscripturally divorced" are still in the marriage bond. He or she cannot have it both ways. If an "unscripturally divorced" person is unmarried, then the divorce breaks the marriage bond. If the bond of the "unscripturally divorced" is not broken, then they are not unmarried. A person cannot be married and unmarried to the same person at the same time. That would be an absurdity such as saying a person is dead and not dead at the same time. It violates the logical principle of the excluded middle. The traditional view requires the word "unmarried" to mean "married and unmarried" to the same person at the same time, which is not possible. They are either married or not married. If "unmarried" has the same application in verse 8 as it does in verse 11, then you have Paul contradicting himself within the span of four verses. If one says a person who is

---

172 Greek word and underlining added.

unmarried is not free to marry another then he/she contradicts the meaning of "unmarried" (not married), and Paul's use of the word in verse 8. The only thing that prevents this woman from being able to marry another is the fact she is still married to her husband, but she cannot be "still married" and "not married" to her husband at the same time (which would be the case if "unmarried" was in reference to her husband)! "Unmarried" must be in reference to someone other than her husband. Remember earlier we noticed that the word unmarried *"agamos"* can mean either "the unmarried state" or "the act of not entering into marriage with someone." It is possible to be married to one person and unmarried in relation to another at the same time! In 1 Corinthians 7:11 the word "unmarried" is being used in reference to others. Paul is saying "if you are married and become separated, remain unmarried in relation to other men." In other words, "stay married to the husband you now have and do not seek to be married to another man (i.e. remain unmarried)." "Do not divorce the husband you now have, but rather seek to be reconciled with the husband you now have."

Those who take the traditional view will claim Paul is saying "unmarried" in the sense that she is unmarried in the eyes of men, not in the eyes of God. It is interesting to me that traditionalists claim that Jesus is saying that a man who divorces his wife for a cause other than adultery in Matthew 19 is referring to how man sees it, not how God sees it, and when they are challenged to prove this assumption, they will refer to 1 Corinthians 7:10 and 11. They do not realize this is a clear case of circular reasoning. Consider this line of reasoning:

Question: *How do you know that Jesus in Matthew 19 is talking about how man sees it, not how God sees it?* Answer: Because in 1 Corinthians 7:11 the woman is told to remain "unmarried." Question: *If the woman who is "unscripturally divorced"[173] is still married to her husband, how can she be unmarried?* Answer: She is only unmarried in the eyes of man, not in the eyes of God. Question: *How do you know she is only*

---

173 1 Corinthians 7:11 would have to be referring to an "unscriptural divorce" because the traditionalists claim a scripturally divorced person could remarry and would not be required to remain unmarried.

unmarried in the eyes of man, not in the eyes of God? Answer: Because Jesus said in Matthew 19 a woman "unscripturally divorced" is not divorced in the eyes of God, only in the eyes of man, and is still married to her husband.

Another reason I do not believe these passages are referring to a divorce situation is because Paul said the woman was to "be reconciled to her husband." He did not say "remarry" but "be reconciled."[174] He did not say her <u>former</u> husband, but to the one who <u>is</u> her husband. Some have claimed that Paul was using a figure of speech. My question is: *Why should we understand this statement to be a figure of speech?* The only reason for assigning a figure of speech to this statement is because it is necessary to uphold a position already arrived at before coming to the verse. Why not accept the plain language and the statement just as it is stated? Another reason I believe Paul was using literal language when he referred to her husband is the use of the word "reconcile." Concerning the word "reconcile," notice the apostle calls for reconciliation, not remarriage.

S. T. Bloomfield *(The Greek New Testament)* says:

> From the use of the word katall [reconcile] and the air of the context, it is plain that the apostle is not speaking of formal divorces, affected by law, but separations whether agreed on or not, arising from misunderstandings or otherwise.[175]

Olan Hicks says:

> What is clearly in view in the divine concern in this entire matter is the sanctity and quality of the husband-wife relationship in marriage, not the legal technicalities of divorce proceedings, not the question of "eligibility" for marriage, not the question of penalties to be assigned or rights to be forfeited, but simply the quality of the relationship and loyalty to it. There is no evidence that God is concerned

---
174 Thayer says the word "reconcile" in this passage means "let her return into harmony with her husband." Joseph Henry Thayer, *GREEK-ENGLISH LEXICON of the NEW TESTAMENT* (1977), 333.
175 S. T. Bloomfield, *THE GREEK NEW TESTAMENT with ENGLISH NOTES in two volumes*, (Philadelphia: Clark & Hesser, 1854), vol. 2, 177.

at all about who may "qualify as eligible to have a marriage... But all the Biblical evidence indicates that God is very concerned with how we treat each other and with the kind of relationship we produce in our usage of marriage. This text, 1 Corinthians 7:10-11 reflects that concern and the word *katallageto*, "be reconciled," particularly reflects it.[176]

A major problem in understanding this passage is the influence of the traditional view. The traditional view causes us to see every passage dealing with marriage as a marriage eligibility passage. I have been told this passage is saying the only person this woman may marry is her husband. Think about that statement; why would Paul tell this woman she may only marry her husband? She is already married to her husband. This passage is not about who this woman is eligible to marry, but about preserving the marriage she has. These passages (verses 10 and 11) are not dealing with this woman's eligibility to marry another in the event her marriage should end or be terminated. What does Paul say about this woman's ability to marry another in the event her husband should die? Not a word; Paul is not speaking to that issue. What does Paul say about this woman's ability to marry another in the event her husband divorces her? Not a word; Paul is not speaking to that issue. What does Paul say about this woman's ability to marry another in the event she divorces her husband? Not a word; Paul is not speaking to that issue. What Paul is dealing with, here in these verses, is the preserving of her marriage. He is telling this married woman to stay married to her husband.

Paul has already dealt with those who no longer have a marriage in verses eight and nine. According to what Paul said in verses eight and nine, if her husband dies, she may marry another. If her husband divorces her, ending the marriage, she is free to marry another. If she divorces her husband, she is free to marry another. If she divorces her husband, ending the marriage, she is free to marry another, but she would not be free from the guilt of breaking her marriage. She must deal

---

[176] Hicks, *WHAT THE BIBLE SAYS ABOUT MARRIAGE, DIVORCE, & REMARRIAGE*, 136.

with the sin of marriage-breaking on God's terms, just as we do with all sins we commit. For example, if a woman murders her husband, ending her marriage, she is free to marry another, but she is not free from the guilt of murder. She must deal with the sin of murder on God's terms, just as we do with all sins we commit. The purpose of Paul's statements is first, to prevent the woman from breaking her marriage. Second, if she does break her marriage, the purpose is to caution her not to end the marriage (i.e. divorce), leaving open the possibility of reconciliation. Preserving the marriage is the point of Paul's statements in these passages. Who or if she may marry in the event the marriage ends is not the subject of verses 10 and 11. It is the subject of verses 8 and 9.

Another word of interest is the word "remain." This word is from the Greek *meno*. How long does one have to remain unmarried, provided reconciliation does not take place? Do they have to remain unmarried for the rest of their life? This word does not in itself designate any specific time span. Unless a specific time is stated in connection with this word, the length of time is not specified. For example in -

John 6:27 **"Do not labor for the food which perishes, but for the food which endures** *(meno)* **to everlasting life, which the Son of Man will give you, because God the Father has set His seal on Him."** (NKJV)

Here we have the word "everlasting" in connection to *"meno"* which gives us a specified time frame. But then you have a passage such as:

Luke 10:7 **"And remain** *(meno)* **in the same house, eating and drinking such things as they give, for the laborer is worthy of his wages. Do not go from house to house.** (NKJV)

Did Jesus mean for His disciples to remain in the house for the rest of their lives? Of course not, but rather they were to remain there for a sufficient amount of time to accomplish their appointed mission or goal, which would require a judgment call by the disciples. In 1 Corinthians 7, this word occurs without a specific length of time specified. The purpose of the remaining unmarried was to save the marriage. The word "remain" should not be pressed into service beyond the scope of the circumstance presented in the context i.e. the hope of saving the marriage. The traditionalist try to require an unconditional "forever" meaning to this word, but they must relinquish their position when one points out that the word "remain" would not mean forever in the case her husband should die. So even the traditionalist would have to admit that "remain" does not mean "remain the rest of her life"! The context requires the woman who has departed from her husband to keep the possibility of reconciliation open by not marrying another. She is not to have a disposition of mind that wants to divorce her husband to seek another. As long as the possibility of reconciliation exists, the woman should seek to remain unmarried in regards to other men. In this case, one of two things will happen. They will either reconcile, or a point will be reached in which reconciliation becomes unattainable. In this case, the only thing left to do is to officially end the marriage with a writing of divorcement so that they can officially end the marriage and move on. The writing of divorcement does not change the fact that the sin of marriage-breaking has taken place. The writing of divorce neither condones nor condemns the sin of marriage-breaking. God gave the writing of divorce as a means of recovery in the event of the sin of marriage-breaking. Many of God's laws were of this nature; that is, they were given to provide a means of recovery in the event of sin. Because God provides a means of recovery in the event of sin does not mean God will not hold people responsible for their sins. The means given for recovery are simply a remedy from God born out of the weakness of humanity.

What about the last part of verse 11; what is Paul saying to the husband? The NKJV says **and a husband is not to divorce his wife.** The question that is central to a proper understanding of this portion of the passage is whether "divorce" is the best translation of the Greek word *aphienai*. This word in its various forms is found in 133 passages in the KJV and not once is it translated "divorce." Mounce does not give divorce as the meaning of this word.[177] Thayer does not define *aphienai* as "divorce," but says the word means to abandon or leave behind and gives Mathew 26:56, Mark 14:50, and John 4:28 as references to this meaning.[178] Strong's does not give "divorce" as a meaning of this word.[179] In this context Paul is telling any man whose wife has left him not to abandon or forsake his wife i.e if the wife has separated herself from you, do not close the door behind her, but leave it open so reconciliation can take place. Wycliff has the best translation in this context **and the hosebonde forsake not the wijf.** (WYCLIFF'S [1385]). Paul is certainly telling the husband not to seek an end to the marriage (i.e. divorce), but more than that he is telling the husband not to give up on the marriage; rather he is to have a disposition open to reconciliation. Both the believing husband and wife are accountable to God to preserve the marriage.

One other point of interest I would like to address before moving on to another passage: the question of why Paul directed this admonition to the women. We could speculate as to why; for example, it could have been because the question of separating may have come from a woman (see verse one). It could be that because the Jewish woman could not divorce their husbands, this would not have been an issue that pertained to women before. This passage certainly suggests women could, under the NT, divorce their husbands, and this new freedom may have been the reason for Paul addressing the women, that is, to curb any abuses of this newly acquired freedom. They too would be subject to the admonition of Jesus, "let not man put asunder what God has joined together." There are other passages in this chapter that suggest women under the NT could divorce their husbands.

<u>1 Corinthians 7</u>:12-15 **12 But to the rest I, not the Lord, say:**

---
[177] See William D. Mounce, THE ANALYTICAL LEXICON TO THE GREEK NEW TESTAMENT, 108, 109.
[178] Joseph Henry Thayer, GREEK-ENGLISH LEXICON of the NEW TESTAMENT (Grand Rapids, Michigan: Baker Book House, 1977), 89.
[179] STRONG'S EXHAUSTIVE CONCORDANCE OF THE BIBLE, Dictionary of the Hebrew Bible, Dictionary of the Greek Testament, 17.

If any brother has a wife who does not believe, and she is willing to live with him, let him not divorce her. 13 And a woman who has a husband who does not believe, if he is willing to live with her, let her not divorce him. 14 For the unbelieving husband is sanctified by the wife, and the unbelieving wife is sanctified by the husband; otherwise your children would be unclean, but now they are holy. 15 <u>But if the unbeliever departs, let him depart; a brother or a sister is not under bondage in such cases. But God has called us to peace.</u> (NKJV)[180] This passage is relatively self-explanatory and would not require much explanation except for the fact that the traditional view has clouded the passage in order to support the position taken on the meaning of Jesus' statement in Matthew 19. Since this passage, taken as it is plainly stated, contradicts the view already held by the traditionalist concerning adultery as the only cause by which one my "scripturally divorce," the traditionalist then must conclude the passage does not say what it plainly says. Because Paul has been recommending celibacy (reason being the present distress, see verse 26), it would be natural for those married to unbelievers to ask if they should stay married to the unbeliever (see verse 1). Paul says if the unbeliever is willing to stay, the believer should not depart from the unbeliever, which was a departure from the Law (see Ezra 10:3). However, this passage suggests that if an unbeliever leaves, then a believing woman (or Man) is set at liberty. So Paul is saying (in verses 10,11) a woman who separates from her husband should remain unmarried in relation to other men <u>for as long as there is any hope of reconciliation</u> with her husband, and the husband should not seek a divorce in the case he becomes separated so that reconciliation remains possible. But in the case of an unbeliever departing, <u>the hope of reconciliation likely does not exist</u>. The unbeliever would not consider himself amenable to Christ's admonition to remain unmarried or be reconciled, especially if the unbeliever was a gentile, since by departing he would consider himself divorced.[181] Therefore, the believing woman

---
180 Underlining added for emphasis.
181 Although the unbeliever does not consider himself responsible toward God, he is, and will be, held accountable to God for breaking his marriage covenant. His being an unbeliever does not exempt him

is not charged with seeking reconciliation nor is she charged with remaining unmarried. The reason may be because the option of reconciliation is likely off the table. It would be almost as futile to tell a believing woman to remain unmarried or be reconciled to an unbelieving husband who had departed as it would be to tell her to remain unmarried or be reconciled to a husband who had died. The possibility of reconciliation in the case of the former would be highly unlikely and in the case of the latter impossible. If, however, she thinks there is a possibility of reconciliation, she may remain unmarried and seek reconciliation, but she is not bound to seek reconciliation simply because it may not be an option open to her.

Those who take the traditional view make some arguments using the Greek to say "not under bondage" does not mean the woman is free to remarry. I am not a Greek scholar but with the help of some Greek scholars and by comparing similar Greek construction in the NT, I think we can show these arguments offered will not stand up to examination.

Objection number one:

The word translated "under bondage" is dedoulotai, and is perfect passive indicative. The usage of the perfect tense verb with a negative particle reveals that one is not now, and has never been under bondage to his/her spouse. (Marriage is not a form of slavery – bondage.)

Response:

H.P.V. Nunn says:

> The main uses of the perfect tense in the New Testament are as follows: (1) The Perfect of completed Action denoting an action completed in past time the results of which still remain.[182]

The problem with the traditional argument is the negative particle does not negate the past action, but rather it negates the

---

from Christ's admonition "...What therefore God hath joined together, let not man put asunder" (Matthew 19:6b). Also see 1 Corinthians 6: 9-11.
182 H. P. V. Nunn, *A SHORT SYNTAX OF NEW TESTAMENT GREEK*, 48.

abiding result, i.e. the bondage.

R. L. Roberts says concerning the Greek in this passage:

> *Dedoulotai* is the perfect passive indicative form of *douloo*, to enslave, and with the negative means literally "does not remain a slave." This is the perfect of existing condition indicating that the party "has been enslaved."[183]

To say the Christian is not under bondage because they have never been under bondage ignores the qualifying phrase "in such cases." If the case is she is not under bondage and has never been, then her case would not differ from any or all cases of marriage, and the statement "in such cases" would be superfluous. Obviously, the bondage in question is only negated in certain circumstances. The only circumstance in view is the departing unbeliever. The perfect indicative expresses the present result of a past action or event. The action in context is the departing of the unbeliever and the result is that the believer is not under bondage. The believer was released from bondage at the point the unbeliever departed, and as a result, he or she remains not under bondage. To say the Christian is not under bondage because they have never been under bondage makes the statement "in such cases" meaningless.

John Murray says:

> The use of the perfect tense should not be overlooked; it contemplates a condition resultant upon a past action.[184]

The past action in this context is the departing of the unbeliever, and the resultant condition is that the bondage is negated, therefore, the believer is not under bondage when this happens. If the believer is not under bondage in the case the unbeliever departs, the antithesis would be: if the unbeliever does

---

[183] R. L. Roberts, "1 Corinthians 7:10-17a," under "Exegesis of Difficult Passages," in 1978: Abilene Christian College Bible Lectures - Full Text: Spirituality, 110-136, published as part of a series called Lectureship Books, (Abilene, TX: Abilene Christian University Book Store, 1978), digitized and made available online at URL: http://digitalcommons.acu.edu/sumlec_man/44/ (accessed 7/7/17), page on electronic document 126.

[184] John Murray, *DIVORCE*, (Phillipsburg, New Jersey: Presbyterian and Reformed Publishing Co., 1961), 75.

not depart, the believer is under bondage. Notice this passage in the same context: 1 Corinthians 7:27 **Art thou bound unto a wife? seek not to be loosed.** The word "bound" is *dedesai*, perfect passive indicative of *deô*. Paul is not saying "he that is bound unto a wife has always been bound unto a wife"! Obviously the word "bound" is referring to when the man married his wife.

Objection number two:

The word douloo never refers to marriage unless this is the one and only exception.

Response:

Would the fact that the word *douloo* refers to marriage only one time mean it does not refer to marriage at all? The argument being made is the word *douloo* never refers to marriage unless 1 Corinthians 7:15 is the exception, therefore implying the word *douloo* may not refer to marriage at all. This line of reasoning lacks merit in my opinion. Upon what is this claim based? What rule of hermeneutics would require such a conclusion? How many times does a word have to be used in a particular way to establish that way as valid? There is nothing inherent in the word *douloo* that would prohibit or allow its use in regards to marriage, it simply means "bondage." The use of this word, as well as most words in scripture, is determined by context. Context is the primary arbiter as to word usage. This word is only found eight times in the NT, so it would not be surprising to find the word being used in reference to something only once, considering its limited occurrence in scripture. This word is used only once in reference to a people being physically forced into bondage (Acts 7:6). In all other instances the bondage is voluntary. Is there any significance to the fact it refers to forced bondage in only one place? No, not at all. It refers to being addicted to wine in only one place (Titus 2:30). It is used twice in reference to one person voluntarily placing himself under bondage to another person (1 Corinthians 9:19 and 1 Corinthians 7:15). It refers to bondage to sin in general in three places (Romans 6:18, Galatians 4:3, and 2 Peter 2:19). It refers to being in bondage to God in two places (Romans 6:18 and Romans 6:22).

The word *douloo* is from the word *doulos* and the word *doulos* is used in reference to Christians being servants or slaves to Christ. The Christian is also described as being married to Christ (Romans 7 and Ephesians 5). In fact, Christians are called slaves of Christ in the very context of 1 Corinthians 7 in verse 22 **For he who is called in the Lord while a slave is the Lord's freedman. Likewise he who is called while free is Christ's slave** *(doulos)*. (NKJV)

Also, in the same context, Christians are called the bride of Christ (Revelations 21:2, 21:9, 22:17) and servants *(doulos)* of Christ (Revelations 22:6). In logic, when two things are equal to the same thing, they are equal to each other. Being a servant (i.e. in bondage) to Christ is equal to being the bride of Christ. From these passages we can see that marriage being a type of bondage *(doulos)* is a concept set forth in scripture.

Objection number three:

The fact that Paul used the word dedoulotai in 1 Corinthians 7:15 and the word dedetai in verses 27 and 39 in reference to marriage shows the word dedoulotai is to be distinguished from dedetai. *The word dedoulotai is a harsh form of bondage while dedetai is a milder form, and marriage is not a harsh bondage.*

Response:

Does the fact that Paul used the word *dedoulotai* in verse 15, rather than the word *dedetai* (which is used in reference to marriage) in verses 27 and 39, mean *dedoulotai* speaks of something other than marriage. Why should it? The claim is that *dedoulotai* is a harsh bondage while *dedetai* is a milder form of bondage. However, *dedoulotai* is used in reference to our bondage to God (Romans 6:22) and Jesus says our bondage to God is an easy yoke and a light burden (Matthew 11:30). Would the use of the word *douloo* make marriage a harsh union? The root word of *douloo* is *doulos;* this word is most often used to describe the Christian's relationship to Christ (i.e. servants in bondage to Him). In fact, it is used in relationship to Christ in this very context (22) For he that is called in the Lord, being a servant (*doulos*), is the Lord's freeman: likewise also he that is called, being free, is Christ's servant *(doulos)*. The word *dedetai* is used in reference to the imprisoning of John (Matthew 14:3), the binding of the demon-possessed man in chains (Mark 5:4), and the binding of Peter in chains (Acts 12:6). In 34 occurrences the word refers to disabling someone, hardly a mild type of bondage. Paul is saying if such a thing happens (in such cases) it does not mean slavery for the believer. Remember the Greeks and Romans divorced by sending away or leaving (see Chapter 6 above). As far as the unbeliever is concerned the marriage is officially undone. In such cases how would one compel the unbeliever to reconcile, since according to Roman law the marriage was over and the unbeliever would not consider him or herself amenable to God's Law. This case would be a very harsh bondage, if one is bound to a marriage the other party considered dissolved.

Objection number four:

The phrase "not under bondage" means the believer is not under bondage to give up faith in Christ to preserve the marriage.

Response:

Paul's statement is in response to a question sent to him (1 Corinthians 7:1). It is hard to believe any Christian would even ask the question suggested by this explanation. There are several good reasons to reject such a notion.

First: Paul is not referring to a case where an unbeliever is threatening to leave, but a case where the unbeliever has left! The horse has left the barn!

Second: Would any Christian think it might be acceptable

to God to give up his or her faith in Christ to preserve one's marriage?! The idea God would approve of a Christian giving up his or her faith in Christ for any reason is diametrically opposed to the very essence of Christianity. The plausibility this question was presented to Paul is, in my opinion, remote. Inferring this question may have been proposed is not suggested by the text itself, it is pure conjecture, and introducing something into the text not even hinted at by the context. One would have to assume the only reason an unbeliever would leave is because the believer would not give up his or her faith in Christ. The reason the unbeliever left is not stated. Since divorce in the first century was even worse than it is today in America, if you can believe it, there was little, if any, stigma attached to divorce. As a result, people in the first century divorced for just about every reason under the sun. There is nothing in the text itself to indicate the reason for the unbeliever's departing. If we let the text speak for itself, we have a plain and simple phrase: "if the unbelieving depart." One cannot tell from the text why the unbeliever left in verse 15 any more than one would know why the believer left in verse 10. Although an unbeliever may depart because of the faith of the believer (certainly one possible reason), to assume it is the only reason under consideration appears to be more of an eisegesis than an exegesis of the passage.

Third: Paul said **But to the rest speak I, not the Lord** (1 Corinthians 7:12). Paul said the Lord had not spoken to the things he now intends to address in the verses following. Question: did Jesus have anything to say about the Christian's family relations in regards to his or her relation to Christ?

Matthew 10:36-37 **And a man's foes shall be they of his own household. He that loveth father or mother more than me is not worthy of me: and he that loveth son or daughter more than me is not worthy of me.**

Luke 14:26 **If any man come to me, and hate not his father, and mother, and <u>wife</u>, and children, and brethren, and sis-**

ters, yea, and his own life also, he cannot be my disciple.**[185]

Matthew 10:33 But whosoever shall deny me before men, him will I also deny before my Father which is in heaven.

Jesus spoke with clarity about whether or not it would be permissible to give up one's faith in Christ to preserve his or her marriage. Therefore, "not under bondage to give up one's faith" could not possibly (as I see it) be the subject of Paul's statement unless "but to the rest speak I, not the Lord" has some meaning I am not seeing.

Fourth: The unbeliever, by departing, releases the believer from a particular bondage. The antithesis would be that the believer would be under bondage to give up their Christian faith in the case the unbeliever does not depart. Surely Paul was not suggesting this as a possibility.

Fifth: No other bondage but marriage is mentioned in this context. So why look outside the context of these passages for an explanation?

Sixth: Paul said **but to the rest speak I, not the Lord.** This is said in contrast to what Paul said the Lord said in verses 10 and 11: **Now to the married I command, yet not I but the Lord.** Both are dealing with a departing spouse. If, in the case of a believer departing from another believer, both are under obligation to keep the marriage together, why can we not see Paul is saying this obligation does not exist in the case of a departing unbeliever? We would if we did not come to this verse with our preconceptions. Jesus' teaching was to two believers and He held them both accountable for preserving the marriage as noted in verses 10 and 11. But in the case of a believer and an unbeliever, which Jesus had not addressed, Paul says even that marriage is right, which was a departure from Mosaic Law (c.f. Ezra chapter 10) and commanded the Christian to not leave if the unbeliever was willing to stay in the marriage (verses 12-14). If in the case the unbeliever is

---
185 Underlining added for emphasis.

determined to leave and not stay in the marriage the believer is not under bondage to preserve the marriage, i.e the believer is not responsible or held accountable for the preservation of the marriage. The believer is not held accountable for not preserving the marriage as is the case of two believers, in which case both are held accountable for preserving the marriage, which is consistent with what Jesus said.

1 Corinthians 7:27-28 **27 Are you bound to a wife? Do not seek to be loosed. Are you loosed from a wife? Do not seek a wife. 28 But even if you do marry, you have not sinned; and if a virgin marries, she has not sinned. Nevertheless such will have trouble in the flesh, but I would spare you.** (NKJV)

Most, if not all, understand "bound unto a wife" to mean "married to a wife" and "loosed from a wife" to mean "divorced from a wife," which would be common sense since loosed is opposite of bound. This passage teaches that one who is loosed i. e. divorced from a wife, if he should marry another, "hast not sinned." Those who hold the traditional view cannot accept the statement of Paul just as it is stated, because to do so poses a major contradiction to the traditional position. The common answer to this problem for those who hold the traditional view is Paul is speaking of those who are "scripturally divorced." Paul says nothing about the cause of the man being loosed or divorced, only that if he is divorced and if he should marry, he does not sin. Let me put to rest the notion posed by some that Paul may have been contemplating a man loosed by way of the death of his wife. When Paul said "Art thou bound unto a wife? Seek not to be loosed," he certainly was not suggesting one should not seek to loose himself from his wife by murdering her. This can mean nothing other than divorce because it would be the only other way a man might "loose" himself from his wife apart from murder. There is not a good reason given in the text to suggest Paul has suddenly changed the subject from divorce introduced in the first part of the clause to something else in the second part. He was clearly speaking of divorce when he said "seek not to be loosed," and he was just as clearly speaking of divorce when he said "Art thou loosed." Those who want to make this saying refer to someone who has lost his wife through death must supply a logical reason for Paul changing the subject mid-sentence. Paul has already dealt with the widows (both men and women) in 1 Corinthians 7:9, and deals with a widowed woman in particular in verse 39. He has dealt with married Christians and Christians who have separated in verses 10 and 11. He has dealt with a Christian married to a non believer and those abandoned by a non believer in verses 12-15. He deals with virgin girls in verses 28 and 36. The only thing he has not dealt with specifically is divorce; divorce is obviously the subject under consideration.

This would also be a perfect place for Paul to remind every Christian of the exception clause and point out that it is impossible to divorce a wife for a cause other than adultery. Is it not interesting Paul simply says "seek not to be loosed" (divorced)[186]? Jim McGuiggan thinks so.[187] It sounds like Paul thought a man could divorce his wife, whether it was for fornication or not. The problem for the traditional view is Paul envisions the man in this passage as one who has been the victim of divorce by his wife. The phrase "Art thou loosed" is prefect tense, passive/middle voice (in the Greek) indicating the man was a victim of divorce. A very good rendering of this passage is found in Young's literal translation: 1 Corinthians 7:27 **Hast thou been bound to a wife? seek not to be loosed; hast thou been loosed from a wife? seek not a wife.** (YLT) When Paul says "art thou loosed," those who hold the traditional view would say this is a situation in which a man is divorced from his wife after she has committed fornication. However, why the person is loosed from his wife is not stated, and to say that it is for the cause of fornication is pure speculation. Paul is envisioning an innocent man who has suffered di-

---

186 See William D. Mounce, *THE ANALYTICAL LEXICON TO THE GREEK NEW TESTAMENT*, 305 and Walter Bauer, William F. Arndt, and F. Wilbur Gingrich, *A GREEK ENGLISH LEXICON OF THE NEW TESTAMENT*, 483. Both works give "divorce" as a definition of *lusai*.

187 See Jim McGuiggan, *THE BOOK OF 1 CORINTHIANS*, (*Looking Into The Bible Series)*, (Lubbock, TX: Montex Publishing Company, 1984), 113. McGuiggan takes the traditional view i.e. a man cannot divorce except for fornication.

vorce as a result of actions taken by his wife (according to the passive/middle voice), and if this man should marry, he does not sin! Everyone, even those who hold the traditional view (if they are honest), knows that if the traditionalist were writing to the Corinthians they would not have written this portion of the letter as Paul wrote it. They would have written the letter something like **"Art thou bound unto a wife? Seek not to be loosed** unless it is for adultery. **Art thou loosed from a wife? Seek not a wife. 28 But shouldest thou marry, thou hast not sinned** provided you divorced for scriptural cause, if not, you will sin."

Some take the position that verse 24 is saying those who come to Christ, as a result of their repentance and conversion, are not required to dissolve whatever marriage arrangement was formed before becoming a Christian and those divorced are free to marry. Is it because they have repented that Paul is not requiring celibacy or is it because Paul is pointing out that although he recommends to those who have come to Christ single to remain single (because of the present distress, see verse 26) he also wants them to know he is not making an edict? To clarify his position he tells those who are married to stay married and he tells the divorced and the virgin that they may marry. It is the opinion of this author that Paul is simply emphasizing he is not commanding celibacy but recommending it. What would the virgin have repented of that would qualify her to marry? Would it not go without saying that the married should stay married? Of course it would, but the married might think because Paul was strongly recommending celibacy he was suggesting the married should end their marriages and Paul is correcting any such notion. The virgin might think Paul was indicating it would be wrong for her to marry; here again Paul was correcting any such notion. While Paul recommended celibacy because of the present distress, he wanted to make it clear he was not commanding celibacy for anyone, including those who had been divorced.

Finally: 1 Corinthians 7:39 **39 A wife is bound by law as long** as her husband lives; but if her husband dies, she is at liberty to be married to whom she wishes, only in the Lord. (NKJV)

The first question in need of an answer is: *What law is being considered here?* Some say it is the Law of Moses, some say it is the New Testament law, but I say it is the law in context, that is, the law of her husband. I think we can safely say this is not referring to the Law of Moses since it was no longer binding. It could be the New Testament law; however, notice the absence of the definite article. The NKJV has correctly translated the Greek because the article is not found in connection with the word "law."

The statement of Paul is in regards to a question asked of him (1 Corinthians 7:1). We do not have the question and we need to be careful about supplying the questions which we do not have. This is certainly no place to be dogmatic. From the answer let me give my thoughts as to the question. First, we need to consider the historical context. There were Jews (and not only Jews but others as well) who believed a woman was, in a sense, being unfaithful to her husband if she should marry another after he had died. They believed it was a sign of virtue for her to remain celibate after the death of a husband. This is reflected in a comment by Josephus in *THE ANTIQUITIES OF THE JEWS:*

> Now, Antonia was greatly esteemed by Tiberius on all accounts, from the dignity of her relation to him, who had been his brother Drusus's wife, and from eminent charity; for though she was still a young woman, she continued in her widowhood, and refused all other matches, although Augustus had enjoined her to be married to somebody else; yet did she all along preserve her reputation free from reproach.[188]

For one to marry after the death of a spouse was called "diga-

---
[188] Josephus, *THE ANTIQUITIES OF THE JEWS*, contained within Whiston's THE WORKS OF JOSEPHUS: Complete and Unabridged, Book 18, Chapter 6, Section 6, 489.

my," and was condemned by some Jews, and even continued to be condemned by some Christians in the Christian age in disregard of what Paul said in 1 Corinthians 7:39. For example, Athenagoras (circa 177 A.D.) termed second marriage "specious adultery." Anthenagoras said:

> ...that a person should either remain as he was born, or be content with one marriage; for a second marriage is only a specious adultery.... For he who deprives himself of his first wife, even though she be dead, is a cloaked adulterer, resisting the hand of God.[189]

It is my contention that Paul was answering a question submitted by a woman whose husband had died, and she wanted to know if it would be wrong to marry. Was she still bound to her deceased husband? This was a question submitted by a conscientious woman who wanted to do right by her deceased husband. Paul's answer is best reflected in a couple of translations.

1 Corinthians 7:39 **39 A wife is bound for so long time as her husband liveth; but if the husband be dead, she is free to be married to whom she will; only in the Lord.** (ASV)

1 Corinthians 7:39 **39 A wife is bound to her husband during his lifetime; but if her husband dies, she is free to marry whomever she will, provided it be in the Lord.** (MNT [Montgomery's New Testament])

Let me be clear, this passage is not dealing with divorce, pro or con. This passage is not dealing with what all ends a marriage. Death certainly ends a marriage, but this passage does not say that <u>only</u> death ends a marriage, either explicitly or implicitly. The word "only" is not in this passage, and the context is not about what constitutes viable means by which marriages may be terminated. This passage is speaking to the issue of

---

[189] Athenagoras the Athenian, A Plea for the Christians, trans. B.P. Pratten, accessed online as part of the Logos Virtual Library, Darren L. Slider, editor, chapter 33, URL: http://www.logoslibrary.org/athenagoras/plea/33.html (accessed 7/7/17).

the woman in the case of a deceased husband. To take this passage, and lift it from its context, and force it into service to uphold some agenda is wrong. Doing so is certainly not handling the word of God aright. Whatever one wants to make of this passage, it cannot be understood in a way to contradict verses 8-9, 15, and 27-28.[190]

---

[190] It is challenging, at times, to see these passages in their historical context. The roles of husband and wife in 21st century America are perceived very differently, and sometimes reversed, from those of the first century (and scripture). It is helpful to make every effort to understand the culture of the first century, especially (as in this case) when dealing with texts that are answers to questions from first century saints.

CONCLUSION

In conclusion of our study of marriage, divorce, and remarriage, I would like to end with a quote from Walter Callison:

> Divorce is not the sin. The behavior is the sin. Divorce is a legal process into which the marriage partners may enter *in order to deal with marital failure.* Divorce, that final step of ending a marriage, provides fairness for both parties as they go on from the end of a marriage which has been acknowledged to have irrevocably failed. Divorce, in itself, may actually be a gift of God whereby both parties can begin to rebuild their lives. It officially ends that marriage. it was meant to do so (for the cast out women) when Deuteronomy 24 was written; and it is a legal procedure which can meet a real need today, the need to officially end a marriage that no longer exists…
>
> If your marriage has failed and you are divorced, the failure is probably not the fault of only one partner. In most cases some blame falls on both. God can forgive, but only after honest soul-searching, honest confession, and repentance…
>
> With true repentance, the failure of a marriage, though tragic, can be forgiven just as other failures to meet God's standards for our lives are forgiven. There are no sins too big for God, if we are honest. Marriage failure is not the unpardonable sin. **If we confess our sins, he is faithful and just to forgive us our sins, and to cleanse us from all unrighteousness. (1 John 1:9 KJV).** The good news for divorced people is that this scripture does not exclude what you did to cause your marriage to fail.[191]

In a perfect world, a study of this nature would not be necessary. But we do not live in a perfect world. The only thing

---

191 Walter Callison, *DIVORCE: A GIFT OF GOD'S LOVE*, 106, 107.

left for us to do is to deal with failed marriages in God's way through His word. We cannot ignore those who have broken marriages or those in marriage crisis. In the past we have held fast to our traditions, but when it comes to those who are involved in these broken marriage situations, we have had little to offer and have often left them to dangle in the wind. May God help us to set aside our preconceptions whereby we "shut up the kingdom of heaven against men" (Matthew 23:13). Rather, may He help us to look into the perfect law of liberty and show those with broken lives that God is a God of new beginnings. **The Spirit of the Lord is upon me, because he hath anointed me to preach the gospel to the poor; he hath sent me to heal the brokenhearted, to preach deliverance to the captives, and recovering of sight to the blind, to set at liberty them that are bruised,** (Luke 4:18).

APPENDIX A

Is restitution the same as repentance? Is restitution a sign of repentance? Although restitution is not directly addressed in the New Testament, it certainly is in the Old Testament, and, by examining some of the passages from the Old Testament, we may be able to gain some insight to help us answer these questions.

Isaiah 55:7-8 **Let the wicked forsake his way, and the unrighteous man his thoughts: and let him return unto the LORD, and he will have mercy upon him; and to our God, for he will abundantly pardon. For my thoughts are not your thoughts, neither are your ways my ways, saith the LORD.** Here, the one who repents must change his way to God's way, and God will pardon him. Nothing is said here about restitution. In fact, God says His way is different than man's way. Man's way is the way of payment and making things right by his own might. Notice how this thinking is illustrated in the story of Jonah. God saw that Nineveh turned from their evil ways and began doing that which was good. They did not make restitution, they simply turned from doing evil to doing that which is right (Jonah 3:10). Notice Jonah's reaction as found in Jonah 4:1-3: **But it displeased Jonah exceedingly, and he was very angry. And he prayed unto the LORD, and said, I pray thee, O LORD, was not this my saying, when I was yet in my country? Therefore I fled before unto Tarshish: for I knew that thou art a gracious God, and merciful, slow to anger, and of great kindness, and repentest thee of the evil. Therefore now, O LORD, take, I beseech thee, my life from me; for it is better for me to die than to live.** They did not have to pay or suffer for their evil past, and that just did not set well with Jonah. Was not Jonah's reaction the same as the elder brother in the Parable of the Prodigal Son?

Let us observe the fact that every civilized society has restitution laws. In this country the insurance business is a thriving enterprise because we have restitution laws and means through the judicial system to exact restitution in those cases where we think we have been wronged by another. These laws are not based on repentance. Although someone might seek an apology from another, the laws of restitution are not in place for that purpose, but rather to make one whole who has suffered loss because of the neglect or deliberate act of another. It is no different with the Law of Moses. Israel was a theocracy; therefore, the laws were religious, moral and civil. In the Law of Moses, the laws of restitution varied depending on the motive of the offender. For example, if someone's property was damaged unintentionally, the offender was required to make "simple restitution," that is, repair or replace property (Exodus 22:5-6). If the offence was intentional and the offender was caught with the goods undamaged, he was required to return the goods along with the equivalent value (Exodus 22:4). If the offender was caught and the goods had been disposed of or damaged, the offender had to pay at least four times its value. If the property was difficult to replace, he had to pay five times its value (Exodus 22:1). The most interesting law concerns a situation in which an offender repented and was determined to make restitution. In this case, the offender had to pay for the property plus twenty percent (Numbers 5:5-10). From these passages we learn that the restitution laws had certain objectives. One objective was to making the victim whole again. A second objective was punitive in nature, that is, the laws were given as a means of punishment for wrong doing. Thirdly, they were meant to be a deterrent to repeating the offense in the future. Fourthly, they were given to encourage repentance. Restitution did not require repentance; restitution was required whether one repented or not. Restitution is not repentance and repentance is not restitution. Repentance is about a change of mind or heart in regards to one's view toward the committing of the offence. It is future-looking, meaning one has determined to stop doing wrong and is determined to do right from now on (cf. Ephesians 4:22-29). Restitution laws are given for the purpose of protecting the rights of others. Restitution is a matter of law whereas repentance is a matter of the heart or mind. The restitution laws were not given as a means of atonement for wrong doing. ONE DOES NOT RECEIVE FORGIVENESS ON THE BASIS OF RESTITUTION, BUT ONE DOES RECEIVE FORGIVENESS ON THE BASIS OF REPENTANCE. Restitution does not undo sin nor does it fix sin. Sins are not undone or fixed, they can only be forgiven. If one has repented he/she will have a mind to do the right thing. Sometimes the right thing may involve restitution, but not always. For example, when Paul obeyed the gospel, the right thing for him to do was preach the gospel to the gentiles. It was not the right thing for him to spend his life trying to make restitution to all those Jewish Christians and their families among whom he had done so much damage before his conversion (Acts 26:9-11). We should be grateful Paul did the right thing, for many of us would not be Christians today if it were not for Paul doing the right thing. Finally, ask yourself this question: *In the story of the Prodigal Son (Luke 15:11-32), why is there no restitution required of this prodigal son?* How much are we often like the elder son?

APPENDIX B

The following is from the URL: https://www.ewtn.com/library/councils/trent24.htm[192]

"THE COUNCIL OF TRENT Session XXIV – which is the eighth under Supreme Pontiff, Pius IV, celebrated on the eleventh day of November, 1563...

[Under the heading] DOCRINE OF THE SACRAMENT OF MATRIMONY: ...Since therefore matrimony in the evangelical law surpasses in grace through Christ the ancient marriages, our holy Fathers, the councils,[6] and the tradition of the universal Church, have with good reason always taught that it is to be numbered among the sacraments of the New Law; and since with regard to this teaching ungodly men of this age, raving madly, have not only formed false ideas concerning this venerable sacrament, but, introducing in conformity with their habit under the pretext of the Gospel a carnal liberty, have by word and writing asserted, not without great harm to the faithful of Christ, many things that are foreign to the teaching of the Catholic Church and to the usage approved of since the times of the Apostles, this holy and general council, desiring to restrain their boldness, has thought it proper, lest their pernicious contagion should attract more, that the principal heresies and errors of the aforesaid schismatics be destroyed by directing against those heretics and their errors the following anathemas.

Canons On The Sacrament Of Matrimony

Canon I. If anyone says that matrimony is not truly and properly one of the seven sacraments of the evangelical law, instituted by Christ the Lord,[7] but has been devised by men in the Church and does not confer grace, let him be anathema.

Can. 4. If anyone says that the Church cannot establish impediments dissolving marriage,[10] or that she has erred in establishing them, let him be anathema.[193]

---

192 *The Council of Trent, Session XXIV*, November 11, 1563, accessed on the EWTN.COM website at the following URL: https://www.ewtn.com/library/councils/trent24.htm#6 (accessed 8/30/17). The website acknowledges that the information was published by Tan Books and Publishers, P. O. Box 424, Rockford, IL 61105 and provided courtesy of the Eternal Word Television Network, 5817 Old Leeds Road, Irondale, AL 35210.
193 Some of the canons have been skipped because they do not directly pertain to the subject of MDR.

Can. 7. If anyone says that the Church errs in that she taught and teaches that in accordance with evangelical and apostolic doctrine the bond of matrimony cannot be dissolved by reason of adultery on the part of one of the parties, and that both, or even the innocent party who gave no occasion for adultery, cannot contract another marriage during the lifetime of the other, and that he is guilty of adultery who, having put away the adulteress, shall marry another, and she also who, having put away the adulterer, shall marry another,[13] let him be anathema.

Can. 10 If anyone says that the married state excels the state of virginity or celibacy, and that it is better and happier to be united in matrimony than to remain in virginity or celibacy,[15] let him be anathema.

Can. 12. If anyone says that matrimonial causes do not belong to ecclesiastical judges, let him be anathema.

Decree Concerning The Reform Of Matrimony

Chapter I
The Form Prescribed In The Lateran Council For Solemnly Contracting Marriage Is Renewed; Bishops May Dispense With The Publication Of The Banns; Whoever Contracts Marriage Otherwise Than In The Presence Of The Pastor And Of Two Or Three Witnesses, Does So Invalidly…

The following is from the URL: http://www.catholicapologetics.info/thechurch/catechism/Holy7Sacraments-Matrimony.shtml. [194]

THE SACRAMENT OF MATRIMONY

…Under the heading *Definition Of Matrimony:* "…The words, which obliges them to live together throughout life, express the <u>indissolubility</u> of the tie which binds husband and wife."

…Under the heading *Marriage Is Indissoluble By Divine Law:* "Not only did God institute marriage; He also, as the Council of Trent de-

---

[194] THE SACRAMENT OF MATRIMONY, accessed on the *catholicapologetics.info* website. URL: http://www.catholicapologetics.info/thechurch/catechism/Holy7Sacraments-Matrimony.shtml (accessed 8/31/17). The website lists a copyright date of 2009, but also says "THIS SITE IS CONSTANTLY UPDATED."

clares, rendered it <u>perpetual and indissoluble</u>.' (sic) What God hath joined together, says our Lord, let not man separate.

Although it belongs to marriage as a natural contract to be indissoluble, yet <u>its indissolubility arises principally from its nature as a Sacrament</u>, as it is the sacramental character that, in all its natural relations, elevates marriage to the highest perfection. In any event, dissolubility is at once opposed to the proper education of children, and to the other advantages of marriage."

...Under the headings *Marriage Before Christ,* and further below this heading under the heading *Before Christ Marriage Had Fallen From Its Primitive Unity And Indissolubility:* "It should be added that if we consider the law of nature after the fall and the Law of Moses we shall easily see thatmarriage (sic) had fallen from its original honour and purity. Thus under the law of nature we read of many of the ancient Patriarchs that they had several wives at the same time; while under the Law of Moses it was permissible, should cause exist, to repudiate one's wife by giving her a bill of divorce. Both these (concessions) have been suppressed by the law of the Gospel, and marriage has been restored to its original state."

Under the heading *Christ Restored Marriage To Its Primitive Qualities and further below this heading under Indissolubility Of Marriage:* "The selfsame testimony of Christ our Lord easily proves that the marriagetie (sic) cannot be broken by any sort of divorce. For if by a bill of divorce a woman were freed from the law that binds her to her husband, she might marry another husband without being in the least guilty of adultery. Yet our Lord says clearly: Whosoever shall put away his wife and shall marry another committeth adultery. Hence it is plain that the bond of marriage can be dissolved by death alone, as is confirmed by the Apostle when he says: A woman is bound by the law as long as her husband liveth; but if her husband die she is at liberty; let her marry whom she will, only in the Lord; and again: To them that are married, not I but the Lord commandeth, that the wife depart not from her husband; and if she depart that she remain unmarried or be reconciled to her husband. To the wife, then, who for a just cause has left her husband, the Apostle offers this alternative: Let her either remain unmarried or be reconciled to her husband. Nor does holy Church permit husband and wife to separate without weighty reasons."

Under the heading *The Law Of The Church On Marriage under The Rite To Be Observed:* "Having explained these matters, pastors should next teach what rites are to be observed in contracting marriage. There is no need, however, that we dwell on these questions here. The Council of Trent has laid down fully and accurately what must be chiefly observed; and this decree will not be unknown to pastors. It will suffice, then, to admonish themto (sic) study to make themselves acquainted, from the doctrine of the Council, with what regards this subject, and to explain it carefully to the faithful.

But above all, lest young persons, whose period of life is marked by extreme indiscretion, should be deceived by a merely nominal marriage and foolishly rush into sinful loveunions (sic), the pastor cannot too frequently remind them that there can be no true and valid marriage unless it be contracted in the presence of the parish priest, or of some other priest commissioned by him, or by the Ordinary, and that of a certain number of witnesses."

The Following is from *CATECHISM OF THE CATHOLIC CHURCH,* under the headings PART TWO: THE CELEBRATION OF THE CHRISTIAN MYSTERY, SECTION TWO THE SEVEN SACRAMENTS OF THE CHURCH, CHAPTER THREE THE SACRAMENTS AT THE SERVICE OF COMMUNION, Article 7 THE SACRAMENT OF MATRIMONY.[195]

"...IV: The Effects of the Sacrament of Matrimony

1638 'From a valid marriage arises *a bond* between the spouses which by its very nature is perpetual and exclusive; furthermore, in a Christian marriage the spouses are strengthened and, as it were, consecrated for the duties and the dignity of their state *by a special sacrament.* '140[196][197]

---

195 Catechism of the Catholic Church, found on the Vatican.va website. URL: http://www.vatican.va/archive/ENG0015/__P54.HTM (accessed 8/30/17). The website gives the following copyright information: Latin text copyright (c) Libreria Editrice Vaticana, Citta del Vaticano 1993. It appears that the information was added to the website in 2003. An English version of the Catechism can be found at the following citation: Catechism of the Catholic Church: revised in accordance with the official Latin text promulgated by Pope John Paul II. Vatican City: Libreria Editrice Vaticana, 1994.
196 Underlining has been added in these quotes for emphasis.
197 Italicization added.

The marriage bond

1639 The consent by which the spouses mutually give and receive one another is sealed by God himself.141 From their covenant arises 'an institution, confirmed by the divine law, . . . even in the eyes of society.'142 The covenant between the spouses is integrated into God's covenant with man: 'Authentic married love is caught up into divine love.'143

1640 Thus *the marriage bond*[198] has been established by God himself in such a way that a marriage concluded and consummated between baptized persons can never be dissolved. This bond, which results from the free human act of the spouses and their consummation of the marriage, is a reality, henceforth irrevocable, and gives rise to a covenant guaranteed by God's fidelity. The Church does not have the power to contravene this disposition of divine wisdom.144"

---

198 Ibid.

BIBLIOGRAPHY

Amram, David. *THE JEWISH LAW OF DIVORCE according to the Bible and the Talmund with Some References to its Development in Post-Talmudic Times.* New York City: Harmon Press, 1968 (originally published in 1896).

Athenagoras the Athenian. *A Plea for the Christians.* Translated by B.P. Pratten. Accessed online as part of the *Logos Virtual Library* which is edited by Darren L. Slider. URL: http://www.logoslibrary.org/athenagoras/plea/33.html (accessed 7/7/17).

Barclay, William. *Introducing the Bible.* Nashville: Abingdon Press, 1972.

Bauer, Walter, William F. Arndt, and F. Wilbur Gingrich. *A GREEK ENGLISH LEXICON OF THE NEW TESTAMENT and OTHER EARLY CHRISTIAN LITERATURE.* Chicago: The University of Chicago Press, 1957.

Bloomfield, S. T. *THE GREEK NEW TESTAMENT with ENGLISH NOTES in two volumes.* Philadelphia: Clark & Hesser, 1854.

Callison, Walter. *DIVORCE: A GIFT OF GOD'S LOVE.* Leawood, KS: Leathers Publishing, 2002.

Dana, H. E. & Julius R. Mantey. *A MANUAL GRAMMAR OF THE GREEK NEW TESTAMENT.* Toronto, Ontario: The Macmillan Co., 1955.

Hammurabi. "The Code of Hammurabi." Translated by L.W. King. Found online at the *Yale Law School Avalon Project* website. URL: http://avalon.law.yale.edu/ancient/hamframe.asp (accessed 3/25/17).

Hicks, Olan. *DIVORCE REPENTANCE AND THE GOSPEL OF CHRIST / DIVORCE & REMARRIAGE The Issues Made Clear.* Searcy, AR: Gospel Enterprises, 1997.

---. *WHAT THE BIBLE SAYS ABOUT MARRIAGE, DIVORCE, & REMARRIAGE.* Joplin, MO: College Press Publishing Company, 1987.

Hicks, Olan and Mac Deaver. *Olan Hicks - Mac Deaver Debate On Marriage and Remarriage.* Searcy, AR: Gospel Enterprises; Austin, TX: Biblical Notes, 1995.

Instone-Brewer, David. *DIVORCE AND REMARRIAGE IN THE BIBLE.* Grand Rapids, MI: Wm. B. Eerdmans, 2002.

Isbell, Allen C. *WAR AND CONSCIENCE.* Abilene, TX: Biblical Research Press, 1966.

Jamieson, Robert, Andrew Robert Fausset and David Brown. *A COMMENTARY CRITICAL AND EXPLANATORY, ON THE OLD AND NEW TESTAMENTS.* New York: S.S. Scranton and Company, , 1875 [originally published in 1871]). Accessed online via Google Books. URL: https://play.google.com/books/reader?printsec=frontcover&output=reader&id=gMIVAAAAYAAJ&pg=GBS.PA486 (accessed 3/18/17).

John Paul II (Pope at the time the text was published). *Catechism of the Catholic Church.* Found on the *Vatican.va* website. URL: http://www.vatican.va/archive/ENG0015/__P54.HTM (accessed 8/30/17). The website gives the following copyright information: Latin text copyright (c) Libreria Editrice Vaticana, Citta del Vaticano 1993. It appears that the information was added to the website in 2003. An English version of the Catechism can be found at the following citation: *Catechism of the Catholic Church: revised in accordance with the official Latin text promulgated by Pope John Paul II.* Vatican City: Libreria Editrice Vaticana, 1994.

Jones, Abigail. "DIVORCE IN THE ORTHODOX COMMUNITY CAN BE BRUTAL, DEGRADING AND ENDLESS." Article in *Newsweek,* November 12, 2013. Accessed online at URL: http://www.newsweek.com/divorce-orthodox-jewish-community-can-be-brutal-degrading-and-endless-3082 (accessed 5/10/17).

Josephus, Flavius. *THE ANTIQUITIES OF THE JEWS.* Contained within *THE WORKS OF JOSEPHUS: Complete and Unabridged. NEW UPDATED EDITION.* Translated by William Whiston. Peabody, MA: Hendrickson Publishers, 2008.

Knight, Dan. "What Jesus Really Said: Putting Away the Mistranslations about Divorce." Article found on the *academia.edu* website, May 24, 2010. URL: http://www.academia.edu/3622738/What_Jesus_Really_Said_Putting_Away_the_Mistranslations_about_Divorce (accessed 7/10/17).

Lenski, R. C. H. *THE INTERPRETATION OF ST. MATHEW'S GOSPEL.* Columbus, OH: The Warburg Press, 1943.

Lewak, Doree. "An orthodox woman's 3 year divorce fight." Article on the *New York Post* website under the *Living* section, November 11, 2013. URL: http://nypost.com/2013/11/04/orthodox-jewish-womans-plea-for-a-divorce/ (accessed 6/2/17).

Lowth, Robert. *Isaiah: A New Translation; with a Preliminary Dissertation, and Notes, Critical, Philological, and Explanatory.* Third Edition. Perth: R. Morison Junior for R. Morison and Sons, 1793. Accessed online via Google Books. URL: https://play.google.com/books/reader?printsec=frontcover&output=reader&id=bz5OAQAAMAAJ&pg=GBS.RA2-PA121 (accessed 3/18/17).

Machen, J Gresham. *NEW TESTAMENT GREEK FOR BEGINNERS.* Toronto, Ontario: The Macmillan Co., 1923.

Madsen, John, creator. *JM Latin-English Dictionary.* Found online via *babylon-software.com* website. URL: http://dictionary.babylon-software.com/adulterium/ (accessed 2/9/17).

McGuiggan, Jim. *THE BOOK OF 1 CORINTHIANS, (Looking Into The Bible Series).* Lubbock, TX: Montex Publishing Company, 1984.

McKinney, Jack. Personal letter to Olan Hicks. A portion of the letter is quoted in Hick's *WHAT THE BIBLE SAYS ABOUT MARRIAGE, DIVORCE, & REMARRIAGE.* Joplin, MO: College Press Publishing Company, 1987.

Moulton, James Hope, Nigel Turner. *A Grammar of New Testament Greek.* 2nd edition. London: SIMPKIN, MARSHALL, HAMILTON, KENT, and Co. LIMITED; New York: CHARLES SCRIBNER'S SONS; printed by Morrison & Gibb for T. & T. Clark, Edinburgh: T. & T. Clark, 1906. Accessed electronically via Google Play books, URL: https://books.google.com/

books?id=Be4NAAAAIAAJ&pg=PR3&source=gbs_selected_pages&cad=2#v=onepage&q&f=false (accessed 6/29/17).

Mounce, William D. *THE ANALYTICAL LEXICON TO THE GREEK NEW TESTAMENT.* Grand Rapids, MI: Zondervan, 1993.

Murray, John. *DIVORCE.* Phillipsburg, New Jersey: Presbyterian and Reformed Publishing Co., 1961.

Nunn, H. P. V. *A SHORT SYNTAX OF NEW TESTAMENT GREEK.* Cambridge: University Press, 1912.

Osburn, Carroll D. "Interpreting Greek Syntax." In *Biblical Interpretation: Principles and Practice: Studies in Honor of Jack Pearl Lewis, Professor of Bible, Harding Graduate School of Religion.* Edited by F. Furman Kearley, Edward P. Myers, and Timothy D. Hadley. Grand Rapids, MI: Baker Book House, 1986.

---. "The Present Indicative in Matthew 19:9." *Restoration Quarterly* 24, no. 4 (1981). Accessed electronically via the Abilene Christian University *Restoration Quarterly* archives. URL: http://www.acu.edu/legacy/sponsored/restoration_quarterly/archives/1980s/vol_24_no_4_contents/osburn.html (accessed 2/21/17).

Pius IV (Pope at the time of the council). *The Council of Trent, Session XXIV,* November 11, 1563. Accessed on the *EWTN. COM* website at the following URL: https://www.ewtn.com/library/councils/trent24.htm#6 (accessed 8/30/17). The website acknowledges that the information was published by Tan Books and Publishers, P. O. Box 424, Rockford, IL 61105 and provided courtesy of the Eternal Word Television Network, 5817 Old Leeds Road, Irondale, AL 35210.

Roberts, J.W. *A GRAMMAR OF THE GREEK NEW TESTAMENT FOR BEGINNERS.* Edited by Donald L. Potter. Accessed electronically on the donpotter.net website. URL: http://www.donpotter.net/pdf/roberts_grammar.pdf (accessed 2/9/17), 2014.

Roberts, R. L. "1 Corinthians 7:10-17a." Under "Exegesis of Difficult Passages." In 1978: *Abilene Christian College Bible Lectures - Full Text: Spirituality,* 110-136. Published as part of a series called *Lectureship Books.* Abilene, TX: Abilene Christian University Book Store, 1978. Digitized and made available online at URL: http://digitalcommons.acu.edu/sumlec_man/44/ (accessed 7/7/17).

Robertson, Archibald Thomas. *A GRAMMAR OF THE GREEK NEW TESTAMENT IN THE LIGHT OF HISTORICAL RESEARCH.* Nashville, Tennessee: Broadman Press, 1934.

---. *Word Pictures in the New Testament.* New York: Harper & Brothers, 1930 (the version used may have been updated in 1960). Accessed electronically via *Power BibleCD* software. The citation for *Power BibleCD* is listed below.

Satlow, Michael L. *Jewish Marriage in Antiquity.* Princeton, NJ: Princeton University Press, 2001. This work was referenced in Peter Zaas' article which itself was quoted in Dan Knight's "What Jesus Really Said: Putting Away the Mistranslations about Divorce."

Shank, Robert. *LIFE IN THE SON: A Study of the Doctrine of Perseverance.* Springfield, MO: Westcott Publishers, Springfield, Missouri, Ninth Printing, 1971 (original publication date 1960).

Smith, David E. *The Canonical Function of Acts: A Comparative Analysis.* Collegeville, MN: The Liturgical Press, 2002 (copyright date [originally published 1963]). Accessed online via Google Books. URL: https://books.google.com/books?id=bk8gRelhVv0C&printsec=frontcover&source=gbs_ge_summary_r&cad=0#v=onepage&q&f=false (accessed 3/7/17).

Stagg, Frank. *THE BROADMAN BIBLE COMMENTARY.* Nashville, TN: Broadman Press, 1969, Volume 8, Matthew.

Staggs, Brandon. *Power BibleCD.* Bronson, MI: Phil Lindner, Online Publishing, Inc., 2015.

Stewart, Ken. *DIVORCE and REMARRIAGE.* Tulsa: Harrison House, Inc., 1984.

Strong, James. *STRONG'S EXHAUSTIVE CONCORDANCE OF THE BIBLE, Dictionary of the Hebrew Bible, Dictionary of the Greek Testament.* Nashville, TN: Thomas Nelson Publishers, 1979.

Sweeney, Zachary Taylor. *The Spirit and the Word: A Treatise on the Holy Spirit in the Light of a Rational Interpretation of the Word of Truth.* Nashville, TN: The Gospel Advocate Company, 1875 (this may be the original publication date). The edition quoted is the 2005 e-book from Project Gutenberg's e-book collection. Accessed online via gutenberg.org. URL: http://www.gutenberg.org/cache/epub/15011/pg15011.txt (accessed 4/14/17).

Thayer, Joseph Henry. *GREEK-ENGLISH LEXICON of the NEW TESTAMENT.* Grand Rapids, Michigan: Baker Book House, 1977.

---. *THAYER'S GREEK-ENGLISH LEXICON OF THE NEW TESTAMENT: Coded to Strong's Numbering System.* Peabody, Massachusetts: Hendrickson Publishers, Inc., 2009. Reprint from the 4th edition originally published by T. & T. Clark, Edinburgh, 1896 with Strong's Numbering added by Hendrickson Publishers.

THE SACRAMENT OF MATRIMONY, accessed on the *catholicapologetics.info* website. URL: http://www.catholicapologetics.info/thechurch/catechism/Holy7Sacraments-Matrimony.shtml (accessed 8/31/17). The website lists a copyright of 2009 but also says "THIS SITE IS CONSTANTLY UPDATED."

Turner, Nigel. *A GRAMMAR OF NEW TESTAMENT GREEK.* Volume III, SYNTAX. Edinburgh: T. AND T. CLARK (printed by Morrison and Gibb Limited), 1963. Although authorship of the series of books is attributed to James Hope Moulton, Volume III was written by Nigel Turner.

Vine, W. E. *An Expository Dictionary of New Testament Words: With their Precise Meanings for English Readers, Volume III.* Old Tappan, NJ: Fleming H. Revell Company, 1966.

Wallace, Daniel B. *GREEK GRAMMAR BEYOND THE BASICS, An Exegetical Syntax of the New Testament.* Grand Rapids,

MI: Zondervan Publishing, 1997 (1996 copyright date). Accessed electronically via Amazon.com. URL: https://www.amazon.com/Greek-Grammar-Beyond-Basics-Exegetical/dp/0310218950 (accessed 3/6/17).

Wallace, Foy. *The Sermon on the Mount and the Civil State*. Nashville, TN: Foy E. Wallace Jr. Publications, 1967.

Winters, Chuck. "Biblical Misconceptions about Divorce and Remarriage (The Church Shooting Her Wounded)." Paper found on the *brutallyhonest.org* website. URL: http://www.brutallyhonest.org/brutally_honest/files/Biblical%20Misconceptions%20About%20Divorce%20and%20Remarriage.pdf (accessed 7/7/17).

Zaas, Peter. "Matthew's Birth Story: An Early Milepost in the History of Jewish Marriage Law." *Biblical Theology Bulletin* 39, no. 3 (2009): 125-128. Although it is not certain whether or not Knight quoted this exact article from Zaas, indications appear that Knight quoted an earlier version or copy of this article in his work: "What Jesus Really Said: Putting Away the Mistranslations about Divorce."

BIBLE VERSIONS

Unmarked passaged or passages marked (KJV) are from *The King James Version of the Holy Bible,* KJV 1769 edition, public domain. Accessed via *Power BibleCD* software. See information about *Power BibleCD* in the bibliography above.

Passages marked (ASV) are from *The American Standard Version,* published in 1901, Public domain. Accessed via *Power BibleCD* software. See information about *Power BibleCD* in the bibliography above.

Passages marked (BBE) are from *The Bible In Basic English,* 1949/1964, Public domain. Accessed via *Power BibleCD* software. See information about *Power BibleCD* in the bibliography above.

Scripture quotations marked (CEV) are from the *Contemporary English Version* Copyright © 1991, 1992, 1995 by American Bible Society. Used by Permission.

Passages marked (DBY) are from Darby's Translation, The Darby Bible, A literal translation of the Old Testament (1890), and the New Testament (1884), By John Nelson Darby. Public domain. Accessed via *Power BibleCD* software. See information about *Power BibleCD* in the bibliography above.

Passage(s) marked (ESB) are from the English Study Bible, New Testament, Third Edtition. Littrell, Harold, translator. *The English Study Bible: New Testament.* Ft. Worth, TX: Star Bible Publications, 1994.

Scripture quotations marked (ESV) are from the ESV® Bible (The Holy Bible, English Standard Version®), copyright © 2001 by Crossway, a publishing ministry of Good News Publishers. Used by permission. All rights reserved.

Regarding passages marked (MKJV): Scripture taken from the Holy Bible, Modern King James Version Copyright ©

1962 - 1998 By Jay P. Green, Sr.

Used by permission of the copyright holder. Accessed electronically via http://www.thewordnotes.com/mkjv/mkjv.htm (accessed 3/6/17). For the purposes of this book, the author accessed the 3rd Edition, 1993 of the MKJV via *Power BibleCD*. See information about *Power BibleCD* in the bibliography above.

Passages marked (MNT) are from *Montgomery's New Testament,* New Testament in Modern English, by Helen B. Montgomery, Published in 1924 by Judson Press. The MNT is in the Public Domain. Accessed via *Power BibleCD* software. See information about *Power BibleCD* in the bibliography above.

Passages marked (NASB) are from The New American Standard Bible 1995 Update. For these passages: scripture quotations taken from the New American Standard Bible® (NASB), Copyright © 1960, 1962, 1963, 1968, 1971, 1972, 1973, 1975, 1977, 1995 by The Lockman Foundation Used by permission. www.Lockman.org

For Bible quotations marked (NKJV): Scripture taken from the New King James Version®. Copyright © 1982 by Thomas Nelson. Used by permission. All rights reserved. Accessed via *Power BibleCD* software. See information about *Power BibleCD* in the bibliography above.

Scripture quotations marked (NIV) are taken from the Holy Bible, New International Version®, NIV®. Copyright © 1973, 1978, 1984, 2011 by Biblica, Inc.™ Used by permission of Zondervan. All rights reserved worldwide. www.zondervan.com The "NIV" and "New International Version" are trademarks registered in the United States Patent and Trademark Office by Biblica, Inc.™

For passages marked (NRSV): scripture quotations are from New Revised Standard Version Bible, copyright © 1989 National Council of the Churches of Christ in the United States of America. Used by permission. All rights reserved. Accessed via *Power BibleCD* software. See information about *Power BibleCD* in the bibliography above.

For passages marked (ORACL), quotations are from the Living Oracles New Testament, by Alexander Campbell, 1826, Public Domain. Accessed via *Power BibleCD* software. See information about *Power BibleCD* in the bibliography above.

For passages marked (RSV): scripture quotations are from The Revised Standard Version of the Bible, copyright © 1946, 1952, and 1971 National Council of the Churches of Christ in the United States of America. Used by permission. All rights reserved. Accessed via *Power BibleCD* which also mentions a copyright in 1973. See information about *Power BibleCD* in the bibliography above.

Passages marked (TCNT) are from the Twentieth Century New Testament, Revised Edition, Published 1900-1904 by Fleming H Revell Company. Public Domain. Accessed via *Power BibleCD* software. See information about *Power BibleCD* in the bibliography above.

Passages marked (WNT) are from Weymouth's New Testament, New Testament in Modern Speech, by Richard F. Weymouth, 3rd Edition, 1912, Public domain. Accessed via *Power BibleCD* software. See information about *Power BibleCD* in the bibliography above.

Passages marked (WEB) are from the World English Bible, Public Domain, Dec 2002. More information on this version can be found at http://ebible.org. URL accessible as of 2/9/17 at: http://ebible.org/.

Passages marked (YLT) are from Young's Literal Translation, Young's Literal Translation of the Holy Bible, by J.N. Young, 1862, 1898. Public domain. Accessed via *Power BibleCD* software. See information about *Power BibleCD* in the bibliography above.

www.ingramcontent.com/pod-product-compliance
Lightning Source LLC
Chambersburg PA
CBHW071619080526
44588CB00010B/1196